Caroline Nixon & Michael Tomlinson

Map of the book

	Vocabulary	Grammar	Cross-curricular	Literature	Assessment
Meet Diversicus Page 4	Main character names Describing people	Revision of Level 3			
1 This year's trip Mission: Prepare a holiday planner for this school year Page 6	Months and ordinal numbers Journeys Sounds and spelling: stress in months vocabulary	***might/may*** *It might be hot.* *You may need a strong pair of boots.* **Indefinite pronouns** *everywhere, somewhere, anywhere, nowhere; everyone, someone, anyone, no-one; everything, something, anything, nothing*	***What's the climate like?*** Learn about climates and climate zones The Arabian Desert	***The lion of the seas*** A children's encyclopedia entry Social and emotional skill: Self-confidence and bravery	A2 Flyers Reading and Writing Part 2
2 Our beautiful planet Mission: Write an explorer's expedition diary Page 18	The natural world Animals Sounds and spelling: silent *e*	**Past simple review: regular and irregular verbs; *ago*** *We got here a week ago.* *We didn't visit Uluru.* *Did you go away last month?* ***too* and *enough*** *There's too much plastic.* *There isn't enough water.*	***Save our world*** Learn about endangered animals Animals in Australia	***When Dad lost his glasses*** A poem Social and emotional skill: Showing awareness of how others feel	A2 Flyers Listening Part 2
3 Let's celebrate! Mission: Have a class quiz in teams Page 30	Competitions Music and festivals Sounds and spelling: *b* and *v*	**Present perfect for experience** *Have you ever eaten black beans?* *Have you ever danced samba?* **Present perfect with *just, already, yet*** *I've already taken more than 100 photos.* *I haven't seen the pyramids yet.* *We've just finished in Brazil.*	***Making music history*** Learn about the history of musical instruments Brazilian carnival music	***The local football hero*** A real-life story Social and emotional skill: Resilience and perseverance	A2 Flyers Listening Part 3
	Review Units 1–3				
4 Time of our lives Mission: Write a chain story about a mystery Page 44	Verbs for offers, promises and requests Telling the time Sounds and spelling: alternative spellings for *ee*	**Past continuous** *While I was cleaning my bike, my sister was watching TV.* *I was getting hot when Mum came out.* **Present perfect with *since/ for*** *We've been here since five past four.* *We've been here for a quarter of an hour.*	***Time zones*** Learn about time zones New Year celebrations around the world	***The legend of Mother Mountain*** A legend Social and emotional skill: Understanding how actions can affect the environment	A2 Flyers Listening Part 4

Unit	Vocabulary	Grammar	Cross-curricular	Literature	Assessment
5 Let it snow! Mission: Prepare a TV weather report Page 56	Seasons and weather In winter Sounds and spelling: revision of *-er*, *-ar* and *-or* endings	***will/won't*** *I'll water their garden.* *We won't talk about football.* **Conjunctions: *so* and *because*** *The weather's really cold, so we have to wear warm clothes.* *Today we couldn't go skiing because it was foggy.*	***Spring, summer, autumn, winter*** Learn about why we have seasons Climate in Argentina	***Tomás and the snowman*** A real-life story Social and emotional skill: Showing remorse	A2 Flyers Speaking Part 2
6 Working together Mission: Invent something to help with a job Page 68	Jobs World of work Sounds and spelling: stress in compound nouns	**Tag questions** *You eat everything, don't you?* *You can cycle, can't you?* **Short questions** *'I didn't go to the bank on Friday morning.' 'Didn't you?'* *'It was my twin brother.' 'Was it?'*	***Inventions and robotics*** Learn about inventions and robotics South Korean inventions	***Buddie and Seo-joon's adventure*** A science-fiction script Social and emotional skill: Friendship	A2 Flyers Reading and Writing Part 4
Review Units 4–6					
7 Then and now Mission: Create an encyclopedia entry Page 82	Things in the home Adjectives to describe objects Sounds and spelling: *j* spelling	**Past participles** *seen, found, driven, ridden, taken, broken, gone, left, tried, forgotten, put, stood, fallen, cut* ***be used for/to*** *It was used for cooking food.* *It was used to cook food.*	***Time machines*** Learn about the evolution of objects The pyramids of Ancient Egypt	***The boy king*** A historical fiction story Social and emotional skill: Taking a different perspective	A2 Flyers Reading and Writing Part 5
8 Space travel Mission: Plan a space mission Page 94	In space Adventure words Sounds and spelling: *s* + consonant(s)	***will* and *going to*** *Spaceships will improve.* *Are you going to watch space films?* **Review of past tenses** *Ivan landed his rocket on the new planet. He was turning off his engine when he heard a strange noise.*	***Preparing for Mars*** Learn about space exploration An Italian astronaut at the ISS	***The space blog*** A science-fiction story Social and emotional skill: Managing own emotions	A2 Flyers Reading and Writing Part 3
9 Great bakers Mission: Take part in a cooking competition Page 106	Mealtimes and snacks Cooking Sounds and spelling: *sh*	***It smells/tastes/looks/feels/sounds like …*** *I wanted to know what it tasted like.* *It felt like dry grass.* *It smelt like carrot cake.* *It looked like a nest.* *It sounded like someone playing an electric guitar.* ***make somebody* + adjective** *The smell's making me hungry.*	***How chocolate is made*** Learn about chocolate production Traditional food in the UK	***The gingerbread girl's adventure*** A fairy tale adaptation Social and emotional skill: Being passionate about what you do	A2 Flyers Reading and Writing Part 6
Review Units 7–9					
Word stack page 120					

Meet Diversicus

1 Read and match.

1 Is Diversicus starting its new world tour? — f
2 Is the director making a film about life in the circus?
3 Do Jim and Jenny live in a circus?
4 Does Jim and Jenny's mum work in the circus kitchen?
5 Does Pablo's mum dance in the circus?
6 Does Pablo's Uncle Marc drive one of the big circus lorries?
7 Do Su-Lin's grandparents sing in the circus?
8 Are they going to go to the same places this year?

a Yes, she does.
b No, they aren't.
c No, she doesn't.
d Yes, he does.
e No, they don't.
f Yes, it is.
g Yes, she is.
h Yes, they do.

2 Complete the sentences with the words in the box.

~~dad~~ uncle mum grandparents brother sister parents friend

1 Pablo's ____dad____ is the teacher at Diversicus.
2 Jim's best ______________ is ten and likes drawing and computers.
3 Jenny's ______________ likes science and computers.
4 Pablo's ______________ is an acrobat and a driver.
5 Jim's ______________ is nine years old and likes sport.
6 Su-Lin's ______________ are designers.
7 Jim and Jenny's ______________ both work in the circus.
8 Su-Lin's ______________ is a singer.

DIVERSICUS

1 Read and write short answers.

1 Is Rose going to show the people making the film around Diversicus? Yes, she is.

2 Do all the acrobats work very hard? ____________

3 Do the acrobats need to eat correctly? ____________

4 Is Ivan the strongest man in the circus? ____________

5 Does Pablo want to make a video, too? ____________

6 Are the boys going to get the video camera and tell the girls? ____________

7 Do Fred and May make all the costumes together? ____________

8 Did the children go and see the acrobats? ____________

9 Did Marc catch Lily? ____________

10 Did Ivan say that the children were brilliant? ____________

2 Circle the correct words.

Jenny's Diary

Yesterday, some people came to make a [1]**film** / **present**. Rose showed them around the circus. First, they went to Dad's [2]**kitchen** / **bathroom** and they saw how he makes all the food, which is very [3]**frightening** / **important** for the people at the circus. Pablo decided that we should make a [4]**website** / **video** too, so he got his camera. We spoke to Ivan, who told us he can pull a [5]**tractor** / **suitcase** with his teeth. Then Jim talked to Su-Lin's [6]**grandparents** / **aunts**, May and Fred, who are the [7]**waiters** / **designers** at the circus. After that I spoke to Marc and Lily. They're the acrobats and I said they could [8]**fly** / **bounce**, but really they only jump. Ivan told the [9]**drivers** / **people** making the film they should use some of our film, but Pablo didn't think it was a good idea.

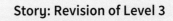

This year's trip

DIVERSICUS

My unit goals

- I want to ______________________________
  ____
- To do this, I will ______________________________
  ____
- I will say and write ____ new words.

My mission diary

How was it? Draw a face.

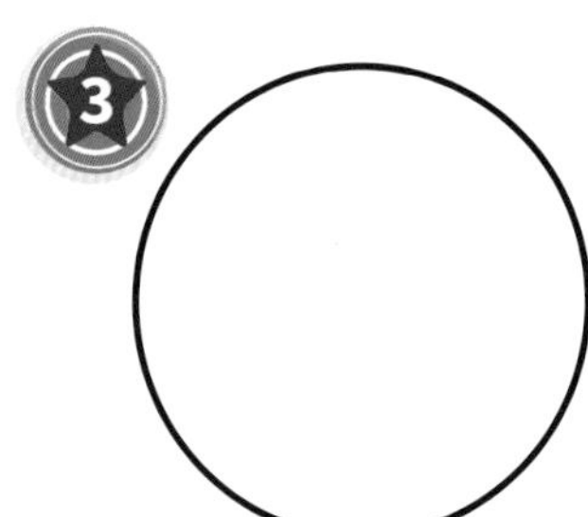

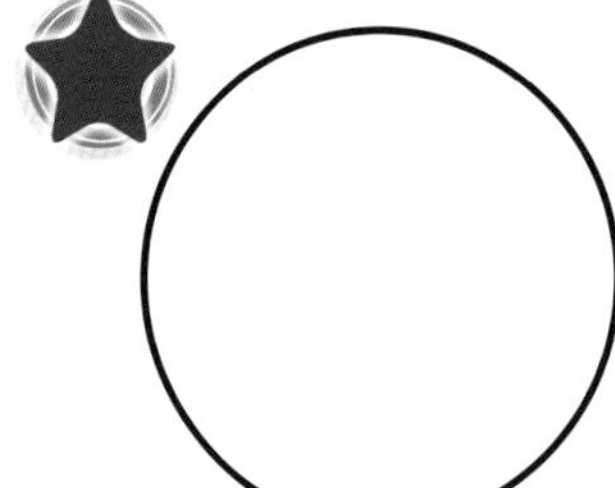

My favourite stage:

____

I can talk about dates and months. ☐

I can talk about possibilities. ☐

I can talk about journeys and transport. ☐

I can read and complete a dialogue. ☐

I completed Level 4 Unit 1. ☐

Go to page 120 and add to your word stack!

1 Read the questions. Complete the crossword.

Across (→)

2 What's the twelfth month?
5 What's the second month?
8 What's the tenth month?
9 What's the seventh month?
11 What's the eighth month?

Down (↓)

1 What's the third month?
3 What's the fifth month?
4 What's the ninth month?
6 What's the fourth month?
7 What's the eleventh month?
9 What's the first month?
10 What's the sixth month?

2 Answer the questions about you.

1 When's your birthday? It's on the ______________ of ______________ .
2 Which month does your school year start in? It starts in ______________ .
3 Which month does your school year end in? It ends in ______________ .

Sounds and spelling

3 4.20 Listen and repeat. Circle the months that only have one syllable.

January February March April May June

July August September October November December

4 Underline the stressed syllable in the other months.

DIVERSICUS

1 Read and write *yes* or *no*.

1 They may go skiing. yes
2 Dubai's got an excellent ski centre. ______
3 They're going to ski outside. ______
4 Jim knows what to pack in his rucksack. ______
5 Jim knows how to ski. ______
6 Ivan thinks the ski trousers look OK. ______
7 Mr Friendly thinks Ivan might need some smaller trousers. ______
8 The man gives Ivan their biggest jacket. ______

2 Put the sentences from the story in order. Write the numbers.

a the other people were unhappy because they thought he couldn't! [ ]

b he didn't know how to ski. Before he could go skiing, Ivan needed to buy some special clothes because he didn't have any. [ ]

c After that, he decided he didn't need anyone's help. [ ]

d Later, when Mrs Friendly invited him to go skiing with the children, he was worried because [ ]

e At first, they all went skiing down the mountain together and Ivan enjoyed it very much. [ ]

f Yesterday morning, Ivan found out there was an excellent ski centre in Dubai. [1]

g Ivan skied down the mountain very fast. He was happy because he thought he could ski, but [ ]

h The man found a very large pair of ski trousers for Ivan and he brought him their biggest jacket. [ ]

3 Review the story.

I think the story is **great** / **good** / **OK** / **not very good**.

My favourite character is ______.

My favourite part is when ______.

1 Read A's questions. Circle the best ending for B's answers.

1 **A:** Can we play a game today?
B: We might play a game at the end of the lesson if …
A we wear striped pyjamas.
B we eat black bananas.
(C) we finish our work.

2 **A:** Where are you going to go on holiday next summer?
B: I'm not sure. We might …
A stay at home.
B take the dog for a walk.
C join the circus.

3 **A:** Who do you think is winning the skiing race?
B: I think it may …
A be snowing.
B be my dad!
C be falling down.

4 **A:** What's the weather going to be like today?
B: My mum said it might …
A be cold tomorrow.
B make a snowman.
C start snowing.

2 Choose four months. What might you do? Write notes.

Jan	Feb	Mar	Apr
May	**Jun**	**Jul**	**Aug**
	party?		
Sept	**Oct**	**Nov**	**Dec**

Now write sentences.

I might have a party in June.

1 Read and colour.

brown plane journey	red ambulance	green motorway
pink platform	orange ship	purple bicycle
hospital	helmet	railway station
traffic	airport	sea

2 In each group, join three words from a word family with a line.

1

January	Sunday	May
November	Friday	August
Tuesday	March	June

2

chemist	train	ambulance
university	platform	bicycle
journey	railway	bank

3

motorway	pyjamas	passenger
umbrella	road	postcard
sandcastle	lift	street

4

airport	traffic	fifteenth
thirtieth	suitcase	app
taxi	lorry	ambulance

1 Complete the sentences with the words in the box.

~~anything~~	nowhere	something	everything
no-one	everyone	everywhere	anywhere

1 I'm hungry. Have we got _anything_ to eat?

2 I lost my glasses yesterday. I looked in my bedroom, the living room and the dining room, but I couldn't find them ________ .

3 I love my new school because ________ is very friendly.

4 I can't hear anyone in the house. No, there's ________ at home.

5 Ow, my foot hurts. I think there's ________ in my shoe.

6 I love travelling because ________ I go there is something new to see.

7 I was really hungry at lunchtime. I ate ________ on my plate!

8 I want to post a letter, but there's ________ near here to buy stamps.

2 Listen and colour and write. There is one example.

1 Colour the map of the world's climate zones.

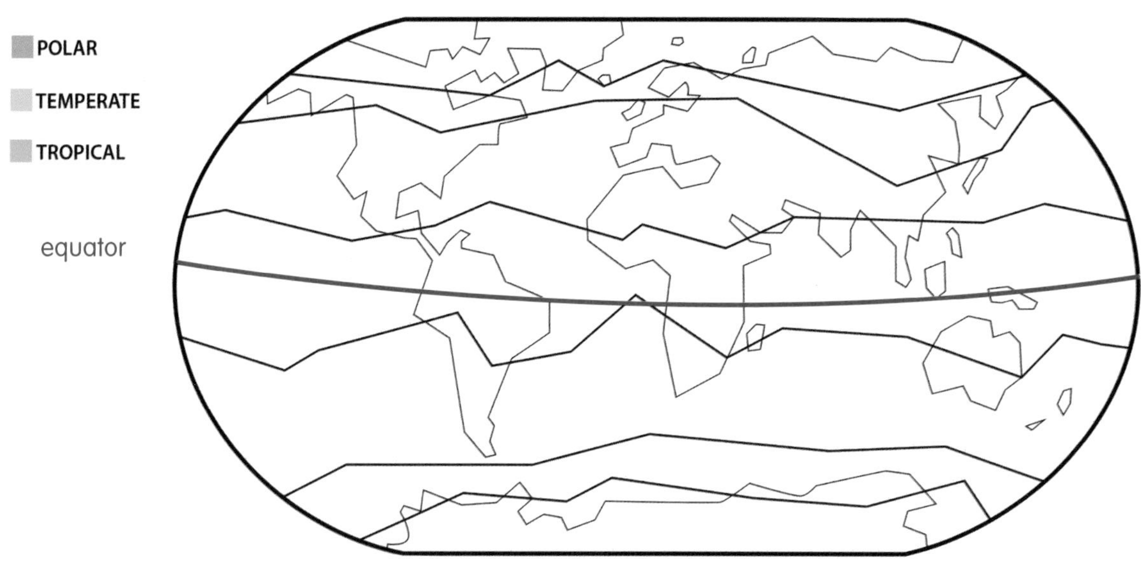

2 Complete the sentences with *Polar*, *Temperate* or *Tropical*.

1 ____Polar____ climates are cold all year.
2 ____________ climates have winters and summers that aren't very cold or hot.
3 ____________ climates are hot all year, but have dry and rainy seasons.
4 ____________ climates have four seasons.
5 ____________ climates are near the equator.
6 ____________ climates are dark all day in winter.

3 Use the internet to help you complete the fact file about deserts.

	Continent	Highest/Lowest temperature
Arabian Desert		
Atacama Desert		
Gobi Desert		
Sahara Desert		
Antarctic Desert		

4 Answer the questions.

1 Why are light colours for clothes better in the desert?

2 Why should you wear long clothes in the desert?

3 What do people in Dubai do at the hottest time of the day?

5 Use the internet to answer the questions about the Burj Khalifa in Dubai.

1 How many floors has it got?

2 How many steps are there to the top?

3 When did they finish building it?

6 Read and complete.

Buildings taller than 300 m are called supertalls and buildings taller than 600 m are called megatalls. Are there any supertalls or megatalls in your country?

Name of building: __________

Height: __________ **metres**

[Find a photo and stick it here]

1 Complete the text with the words in the box.

~~sailor~~ routes stars navigation found explorer

Ahmad Ibn Majid's father was a famous [1] sailor and he taught his young son all about [2] ______. Ahmad Ibn Majid later studied the [3] ______ in the sky and used them to help him find different sea [4] ______ to distant places. He helped Vasco da Gama, the famous Portuguese [5] ______, on his famous journey when he [6] ______ the Cape of Good Hope.

2 Complete the information about Ahmad Ibn Majid.

From:

______

______

Job:

______

______

______

Famous because:

______

______

______

Called:

______

______

3 Work in groups. Choose and research the life of an explorer who sailed to visit new lands. Write a short encyclopedia entry about him.

Ferdinand Magellan Vasco da Gama Marco Polo

Name: ______ **Born:** ______ **Died:** ______

Famous because: ______

______

______

Other interesting information:

______

Read the text. Choose the right words and write them on the lines.

Christopher Columbus was born [1] ___in___ Italy in 1451.

As a young man, Christopher Columbus studied maps and learnt how to [2] ______ a ship. Columbus wanted to go to China and East Asia. There [3] ______ a sea route around Africa, but he wanted to find a new route that was [4] ______ than the one everyone knew.

He left with three ships on 3rd August, 1492. The journey was very [5] ______ and difficult and the sea was very dangerous. On 12th October, 1492, Columbus [6] ______ land. It was a small island. He thought it was the Indies, so he called the people [7] ______ lived there 'Indians'. Actually it was the sea route across the Atlantic to the Americas. The Earth was much [8] ______ than Columbus thought. Columbus went to the Americas three times, but when he [9] ______ on 20th May, 1506, he [10] ______ thought that his journey was a shorter sea route to Asia.

1 in on at
2 sail sailing sailed
3 might were was
4 short shorter shortest
5 longer long longest
6 see seeing saw
7 which where who
8 big bigger biggest
9 die died dying
10 soon once still

1 **Harry is asking his mum about going to school tomorrow. What does she say? Read the conversation and choose the best answer. Write a letter (A–H) for each answer. You do not need to use all of the letters. There is one example.**

Example

Harry: Mum, can you give William a lift to school tomorrow?

Mum: F

Questions

1 **Harry:** Yes, she is. What time should William be ready?

Mum: ______________

2 **Harry:** OK, thanks, Mum. Tomorrow, Mr Young is coming to talk to us about using bicycles on busy roads.

Mum: ______________

3 **Harry:** Yes, he is. His wife was our teacher last year.

Mum: ______________

4 **Harry:** You might see her tomorrow morning at school.

Mum: ______________

5 **Harry:** OK, Mum. I'm going to call William now.

Mum: ______________

A No, because we mustn't be late.

B Oh yes. You have Mrs Park this year.

C Is she a new teacher?

D Please say I hope his mum's better soon.

E Great – I'd like to meet her.

F Yes, of course. Is his mum still ill? **(example)**

G That's good! Is he the husband of a teacher at your school?

H Eight o'clock, please, because there might be a lot of traffic.

1 Read the instructions. Play the game.

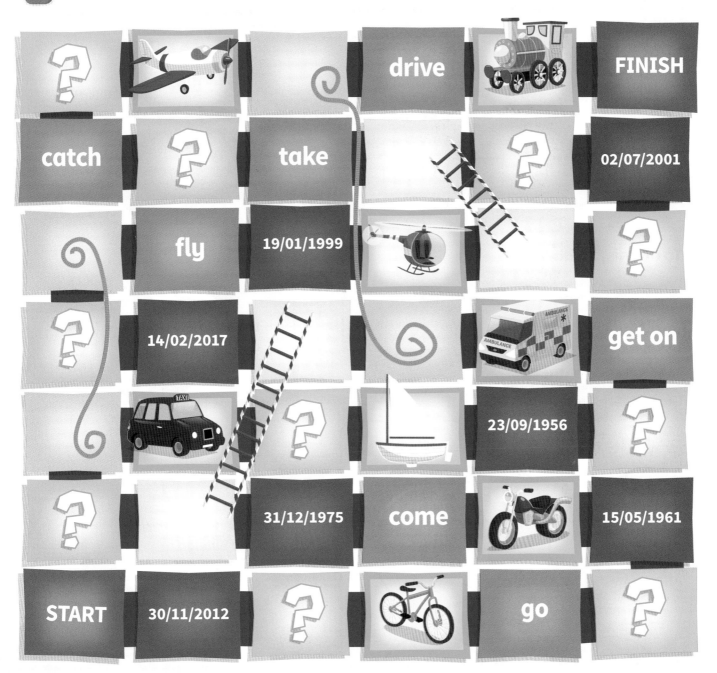

?			drive		FINISH
catch	?	take		?	02/07/2001
	fly	19/01/1999			?
?	14/02/2017				get on
		?		23/09/1956	?
?		31/12/1975	come		15/05/1961
START	30/11/2012	?		go	?

INSTRUCTIONS

Roll the dice and move.

On green squares, say the word.

On orange squares, say the past of the verb and spell it.

On purple squares, say the date.

On ? squares, answer the question on the card.

Go up the ladder. Go down the rope.

Our beautiful planet

DIVERSICUS

My unit goals

- I want to ______________________________
- To do this, I will ______________________________
- I will say and write ____ new words.

My mission diary

How was it? Draw a face.

1

2

3

My favourite stage: ______________________________

I can name places and animals we see in the environment. ☐

I can read and talk about events in the past. ☐

I can use *too much / not enough* to talk about the environment. ☐

I can listen to information and complete notes. ☐

I completed Level 4 Unit 2. ☐

Go to page 12(and add to you word stack!

1 Circle the different word.

1 ocean stream (moon) river
2 land island desert sea
3 wood forest jungle air
4 cave ocean desert hill
5 fire stone hill rock
6 tree forest stream wood
7 waterfall stream land river
8 mountain ocean sea beach

2 Order the letters and complete the puzzle.

1 dtrees
2 dlna
3 vcea
4 llhi
5 ria
6 odow
7 teson
8 mertas
9 rife
10 necoa
11 streof

What's the secret word?

______

1 DESERT
2
3
4
5
6
7
8
9
10
11

Sounds and spelling

3 4.22 Listen and repeat. ~~Cross out~~ the *e* if it's silent.

cav~~e~~ June children motorbike desert zone

4 4.23 Listen and complete the table.

Silent *e*	You say/hear the *e*
stone	environment

DIVERSICUS

1 Read and correct.

1 Mr and Mrs Friendly know everything about the trip.

Mr and Mrs Friendly don't know anything about the trip.

2 They had to look for a shop which sold belts.

____

3 Su-Lin spent an hour writing letters. _______________

4 A bear appeared behind a tree. _______________

5 They saw lots of amazing websites. _______________

2 Complete the text with the past simple form of the verbs.

Jim's Diary

Last week we [1] went (go) on a school trip to the beach. We [2] _______ (leave) after school on Friday, but we didn't get to the beach until eight o'clock. It [3] _______ (take) five and a half hours because we had to stop on the way. I forgot to take my pyjamas and we had to buy some. Then Su-Lin [4] _______ (find) a post office. She [5] _______ (buy) some stamps and then [6] _______ (begin) to write her postcards. She [7] _______ (spend) an hour writing them!

When we [8] _______ (get) to the beach and began to put up the tents, it was dark. We [9] _______ (put) them up OK, but then Jenny heard a noise. She went outside and saw a kangaroo. She [10] _______ (run) away from it, but she ran into Pablo and together they [11] _______ (fall) over and broke the tent. Jenny and Pablo [12] _______ (cut) their knees and elbows, so the next day they both stayed on the beach and I looked after them.

3 Review the story.

I think the story is **great** / **good** / **OK** / **not very good**.

My favourite character is _______ .

My favourite part is when _______________ .

1 Read and answer.

Oliver loved reading books about brave people who sailed across oceans to find new islands, or who stayed for months in dry, hot deserts to study them. One day he read about the first woman who drove across the African desert.

Oliver decided to go on an adventure, too. He went out into the garden and started to think. What did he need for his adventure? Everyone who went on an adventure took food, a rucksack, and a map of course!

He began drawing a map of his garden because he didn't want to get lost. Before he left the house, he told his little sister Zoe about his trip and she was very excited about it. Oliver decided to let his sister go with him on the adventure. It took them almost five minutes to study the garden. They drew some plants and flowers, but then their mum called them. It was time for lunch. They forgot about the garden and their adventure until the afternoon.

1 What did Oliver love reading? He loved reading books about brave people.

2 What did he decide to do? ______________________

3 What did he begin drawing? ______________________

4 What did Oliver and Zoe draw? ______________________

5 Why did their mum call them? ______________________

____

2 Look at the code. Write the message.

a	b	c	d	e	f	g	h	i	j	k	l	m
+	÷	∞	▼	±	>	≠	/	√	✖	⬇	Δ	♈

n	o	p	q	r	s	t	u	v	w	x	y	z
ч	φ	Ω	Σ	♦	▲	◗	●	O	✚	■	★	□

>♦+ч⬇ +ч▼ /+♦♦★ Δ±>◗ + ♈φч◗/ +≠φ. ◗/±★
◗♦+O±ΔΔ±▼ ◗/♦φ●≠/ ◗/± ▼±▲±♦◗, ÷●◗ √◗ ✚+▲
▼√>>√∞●Δ◗. ✚/±ч ◗/±★ >φ●ч▼ + ▲◗♦±+♈,
√◗ ✚+▲ ▼♦★. ◗/±★ /+▼ ◗φ ∞φ♈± ÷+∞⬇.

Frank / ___ / ___ / ___ / _ / ___ / ___. / ___ /
___ / ___ / ___ / ___, / ___ / ___ /
___ / ___. / ___ / ___ / ___ / _ / ___,
/ ___ / ___ / ___. / ___ / ___ / ___ / ___ / ___.

1 Look at the pictures. Complete the crossword.

Across (→)

2 4 5 7 9

Down (↓)

1 3 6 8

1 D I N O S A U R

2 Look and read. Choose the correct words and write them on the lines. There is one example.

an octopus a penguin a camel **insects** eagles

dinosaurs a tortoise a kangaroo

a bear **a butterfly** a swan

This wild animal might live in a cave. It may be very dangerous. _a bear_

1 This big bird is white or black with a very long neck. It lives near streams or rivers. ______________

2 This animal lives in the ocean. It's got eight 'arms and legs'. ______________

3 These animals are extinct. They lived long ago and we can find out about them in museums. ______________

4 These small creatures have got six legs and most have got wings. A beetle is one of these. ______________

5 This green and brown animal is very slow. It's got a shell on its back. ______________

6 This beautiful insect may have a lot of different colours. It's got four wings. ______________

7 These very large strong birds live in tall trees or at the top of mountains. ______________

1 Circle the correct words.

1 I like ice skating, but if you don't wear the right clothes it's (too) / **enough** cold.

2 My sister had a birthday party yesterday and I couldn't study because there was too **much** / **many** noise.

3 Pets shouldn't go near the road. It's **too** / **enough** dangerous.

4 I love going to football games, but sometimes there are too **much** / **many** people.

5 Last night I went to bed and I didn't see the end of the programme because I was **too** / **enough** tired.

6 My mum doesn't want me to walk through the park when it's dark because she says it isn't safe **too** / **enough**.

7 My dog doesn't enjoy going for long walks. He's **too** / **enough** lazy.

8 My dad didn't let me get into the car with my football boots on. He said they weren't clean **too** / **enough**.

2  Read the text. Choose the correct words and write them on the lines.

All of the deserts in Australia are huge. The desert is one of the [1] ___driest___ environments in the world. There isn't enough water and [2] ________ creatures can't live there because it's [3] ________ hot. There's a lot of sun on the sand, rocks and stones during the day and this [4] ________ the temperature go up.

People took camels to Australia two hundred years [5] ________ because they can live in this environment. They [6] ________ live without water for several days. Camels are called 'ships of the desert'.

When people [7] ________ in the desert, they must be very careful. They must take [8] ________ water with them because it might be a long way to the next town.

1	dry	driest	drier	5	after	ago	last
2	much	most	lot	6	can	can't	don't
3	too	enough	more	7	travels	travel	travelled
4	makes	making	made	8	too	enough	little

1 Are these animals *extinct* or *endangered*?

1 Pandas are endangered.
2 Dinosaurs are ______.
3 Gorillas are ______.
4 Elephants are ______.
5 Dodos are ______.
6 Polar bears are ______.

2 Read the problems that animals have because of humans. Match the problems with the animals.

1 Many animals are endangered because hunters kill them for their beautiful fur, shell or skin. a b ☐

2 Some animals eat plastic in the ocean because they think it is food. Others die because they swim into something made of plastic and cannot escape. ☐ ☐

3 When we build roads or cities, we change the place where animals live. This often means that the animals can't live there any more. ☐

a

b

c

d

e

3 Read about the Tasmanian tiger and answer the questions.

1 What did the Tasmanian tiger look like?

2 How did it move?

3 Why are Tasmanian tigers (probably) extinct?

4 Sometimes people say 'I saw a Tasmanian tiger in the Australian desert!' Do you think this is possible? Why? / Why not?

4 Look at the information about kangaroos and platypuses in the Venn diagram. Talk to a friend about how they are similar and how they are different.

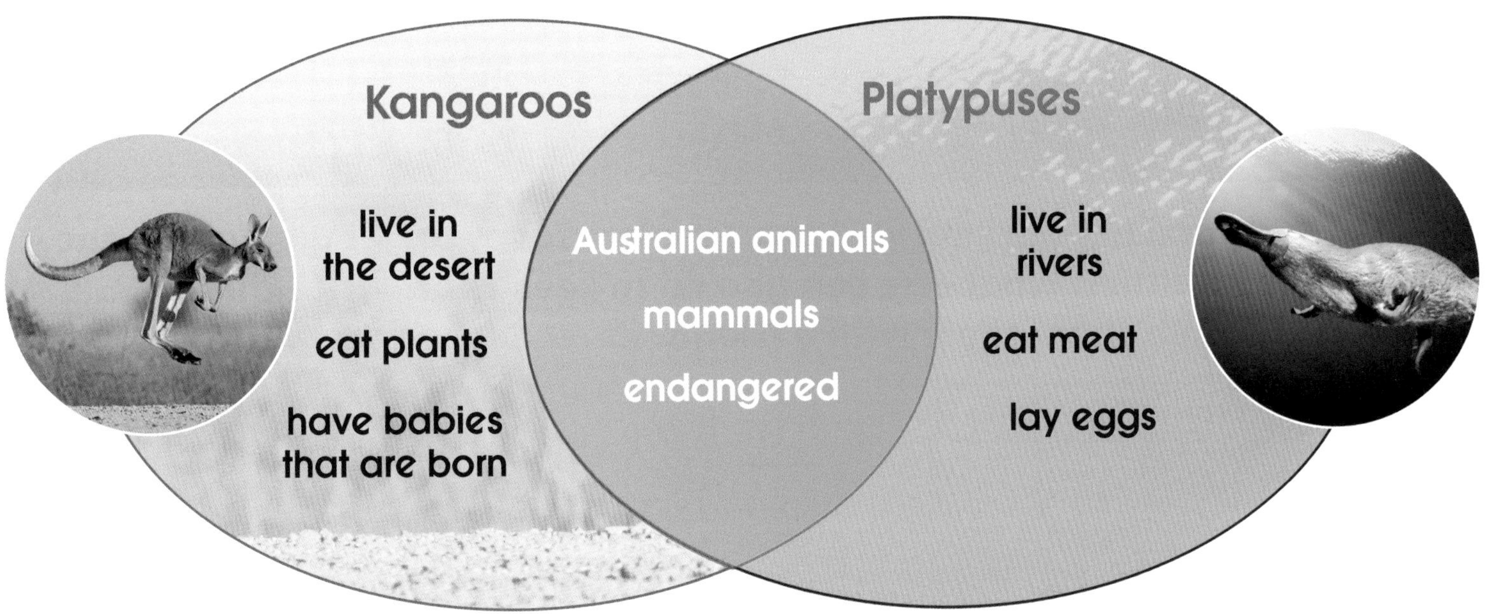

1 Order the events from the poem 1–6.

a [ ] The family visits the Jenolan Caves.
b [ ] Amy's dad loses his glasses.
c [1] Amy and her parents go to Australia.
d [ ] Amy says 'Let's go somewhere cold.'
e [ ] Amy finds her dad's glasses.
f [ ] They say it's too hot for them.

2 Complete the next verse of the poem with the words in the box.

~~caves~~ car dad way far sky day long

When we left the nice [1] caves at the end of the [2] ______
The light from the [3] ______ showed us the [4] ______.
'Were we down there so [5] ______?' my mum said near the [6] ______.
'Hours,' my [7] ______ said. 'We all walked so [8] ______.'

3 Amy and her parents visit the Jenolan Caves to get away from the hot weather. What else can you do to keep cool? Write three ideas and then share them with a friend.

You can go swimming.

______

______

______

Amy is asking her dad some questions about his first trip to Australia. What does Amy's dad say? Read the conversation and choose the best answer. Write a letter (A–H) for each answer. You do not need to use all the letters. There is one example.

Example

 **Amy:** Did you go to Australia when you were young, Dad?

Dad: H

Questions

1  **Amy:** How long were you there?

 **Dad:** ______

2  **Amy:** Really? And who did you go with?

 **Dad:** ______

3 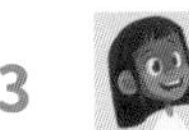 **Amy:** Where did you stay?

 **Dad:** ______

4  **Amy:** That's great. And what did you do there?

 **Dad:** ______

5  **Amy:** Did you enjoy it?

 **Dad:** ______

A Oh, for about five weeks.

B Pardon? Tom didn't go!

C Yes, I did. Tom loved it too.

D My friend Tom – we had great fun!

E You're welcome! Please stay with us.

F Lots of things – one was camel riding!

G Tom's uncle lives in a large house in Sydney. We were with him for a few weeks.

H Yes, I did! I was only 21 when I went there. **(example)**

1 4.24 Listen and write. There is one example.

The World of Animals Museum

	A class visit from:	Castle	School
1	Date of visit:	______	rd May
2	Student's name:	______	Swan
3	Favourite thing:	______	
4	Café:	had ______	to drink
5	Bought a book about	______	

1 Read the instructions. Play the game.

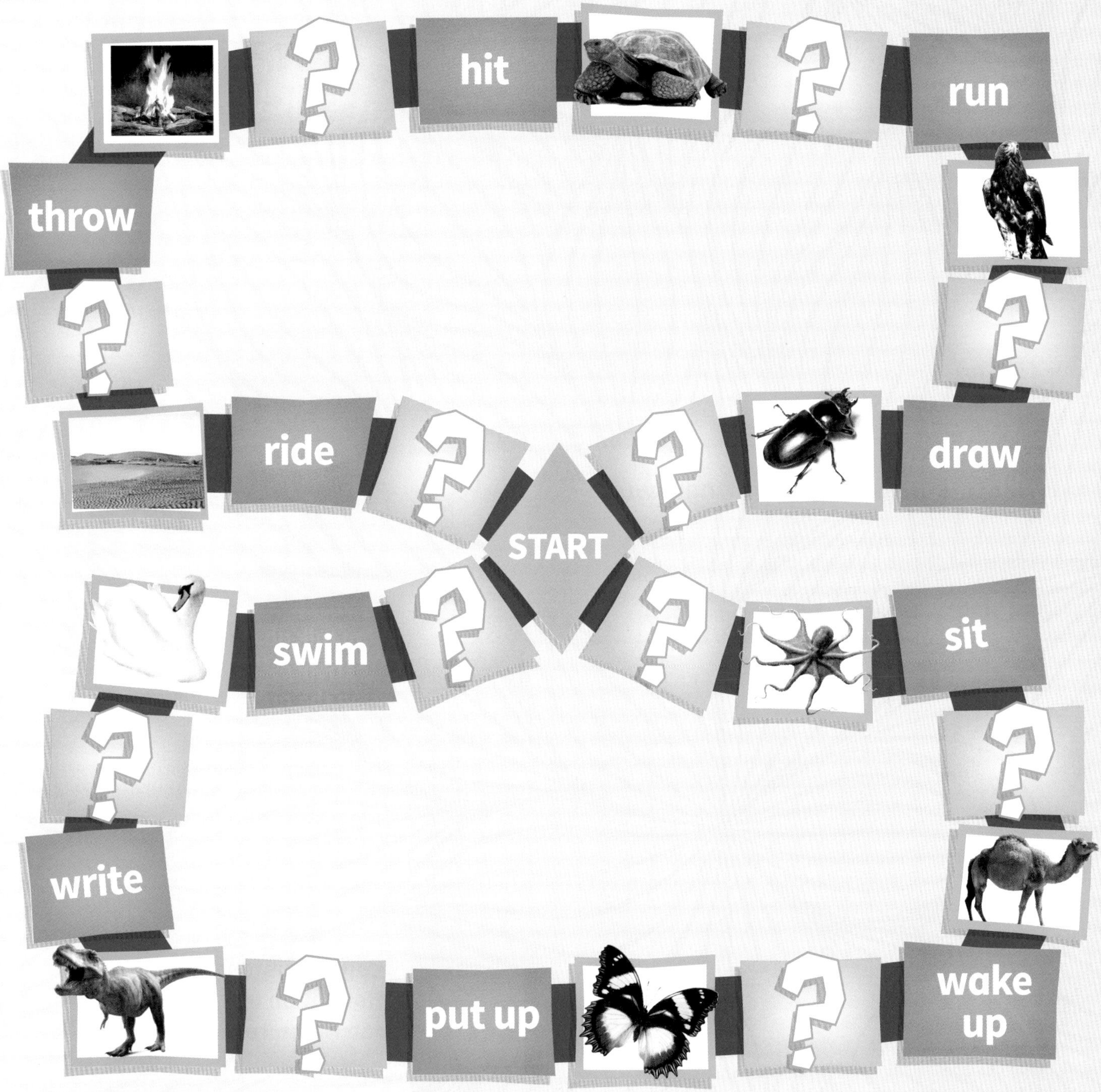

throw

hit

run

ride

START

draw

swim

sit

write

put up

wake up

INSTRUCTIONS

Choose four pictures. Write the words in your notebook. You must collect these.

Roll the dice and move.

Collect your four words. Tick ✓ them in your notebook.

On green squares, say the word.

On ? squares, answer the question on the card.

On orange squares, say the past of the verb and spell it.

3 Let's celebrate!

My unit goals

- I want to ______________________________
- To do this, I will ______________________________
- I will say and write ____ new words.

My mission diary

How was it? Draw a face.

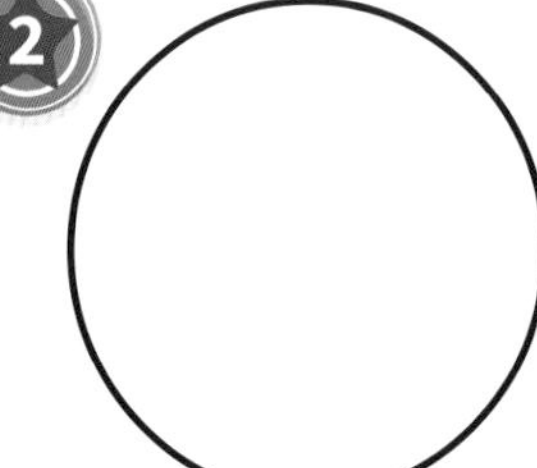

My favourite stage:

I can talk about games and competitions. ☐

I can talk about experiences using the present perfect. ☐

I can talk about festivals and music. ☐

I can understand information to match pictures. ☐

I completed Level 4 Unit 3. ☐

Go to page 12(and add to you word stack!

1 Read and complete the sentences.

1 People drive fast in racing cars to win a race.
2 ________ is a board game with a king and queen.
3 ________ is a popular ball game on the beach.
4 A ________ is someone who wins.
5 A ________ is a group of players who play together.
6 A ________ is a competition with questions.
7 He won first ________ in the painting competition.
8 Can I help you with that crossword ________? I love them!
9 I didn't enjoy that football ________. The teams didn't play well.

2 Read and match. Then check your answers and spelling in Activity 1.

1 Which team won the volleyball match? — b
2 How did she finish the puzzle so quickly?
3 Did he win a prize for chess?
4 Why was he unhappy about the race?
5 Who was the winner of the quiz?

a No, it was for drawing.
b The yellow team did.
c Because he didn't win it.
d Sophia – she knows a lot!
e Her dad helped her.

Sounds and spelling

3 4.25 Listen and repeat. Write the words in the correct box.

b		v	
October			

1 Choose words from the box to complete the sentences. You do not need to use all the words.

~~excellent~~ weekend chess costume sofa Ivan volleyball Jenny
plane king castle Jim queen ice creams lucky

1 Su-Lin says '___Excellent___! Well done!' to Jenny and Pablo.
2 Su-Lin and Jim are playing ___________.
3 Su-Lin can take Jim's ___________ now, so he's lost the game.
4 ___________'s gone to get the volleyball.
5 How many ___________ did Ivan buy?
6 There were four people on the ___________ which Ivan lifted.
7 Su-Lin's seen a photo of Ivan with the ___________.
8 Next ___________, it's Rio Carnival.
9 Ivan's going to wear a king ___________.
10 ___________ lifts a castle, but it's from the game.

2 Read and correct.

1 Jenny and Pablo have won the ~~tennis~~ match. ___volleyball___
2 When someone can take your queen, you lose a game of chess. ___________
3 The ball was above the ice cream cart. ___________
4 Ivan's bought four ice creams. ___________
5 Ivan's ice cream is the smallest one. ___________
6 Rio Carnival's the biggest birthday party in the world. ___________
7 Ivan says he's going to be the king of the carnival. ___________
8 Ivan thinks everyone can lift a castle. ___________

3 Review the story.

I think the story is **great** / **good** / **OK** / **not very good**.
My favourite character is ___________.
My favourite part is when ___________________________.

1 Read the information. Complete the diagram with names A–D and positive (+) or negative (–) sentences in the present perfect.

Four children are sitting at a table. There are three girls and one boy, called Harry. The boy's sitting opposite Katy. They're talking about the start of this school year. What have they done?

Betty's sitting between Harry and Katy. Betty's won three volleyball matches.

Harry hasn't eaten pizza, but he's cooked pasta for his parents.

The child opposite Holly hasn't lost a game of chess.

A girl next to Katy hasn't drunk coffee, but she's seen two eagles.

The girl who's made two new friends hasn't been to the theatre.

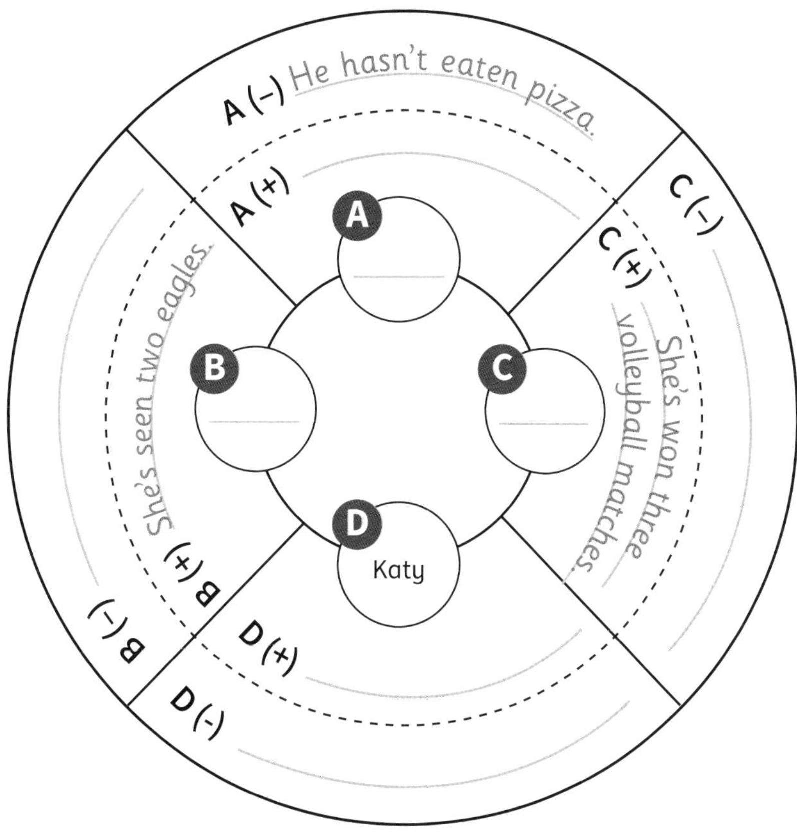

2 Ask and answer with a partner.

~~be~~ see win play travel run do walk ~~competition~~
camel prize chess motorway race crossword puzzle desert

Have you ever been in a competition?

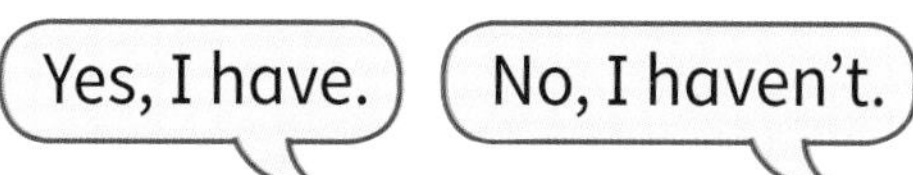

1 Write the words in the correct picture.

~~drum~~ ~~concert~~ ~~prize~~ ~~chess~~ piano volleyball violin rock music badminton stage golf match guitar race musician winner

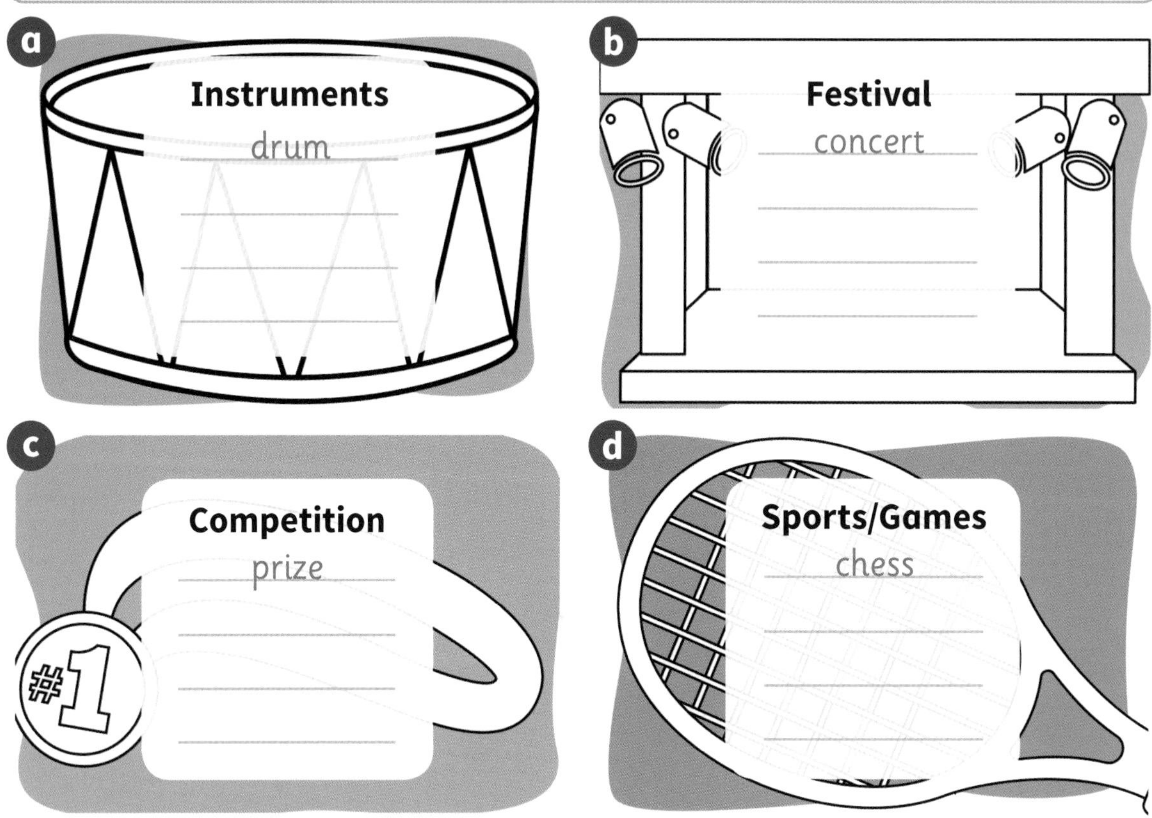

2 Read and circle the correct words.

Last weekend my parents took me to a music [1]**festival** / **traffic** in a field near our village. It was great. There was a small [2]**drum** / **stage** outside where the rock musicians played. The [3]**musician** / **waiter** who played the drums was brilliant. He played really [4]**better** / **well** and the singer sang [5]**noisy** / **loudly** because it was rock music. Dad didn't like the [6]**tunes** / **streams** much. He thought they were too noisy and that the musicians didn't know how to play their [7]**instruments** / **stones**, but Mum loved the [8]**concert** / **match**. She danced all evening, and so did I!

3 Write about a festival in your country.

- Where is it?
- When is it?
- What can you see and do?

1 Put the words in order. Write the sentences.

1 (the email) (I haven't) (yet.) (sent him)
I haven't sent him the email yet.

2 (just) (Frank's grandma.) (visited) (We've)

3 (homework for tomorrow.) (already) (I've) (done all my)

4 (washed) (She's) (her hair.) (just)

5 (you been) (yet?) (Have) (to the dentist's)

6 (yet.) (He hasn't) (breakfast) (finished)

7 (already) (They've) (for lunch.) (bought the food)

8 (the photo) (taken) (yet?) (Has she)

2 Read the postcard and write the missing words.

I've [1] just bought this postcard to tell you about my holiday in Brazil! I've already done a lot of amazing things. I've [2] ______ volleyball on the beach and I've [3] ______ pineapple juice with coconut milk. Yesterday evening, we went to the biggest festival that I've ever seen and it was fantastic. There [4] ______ a lot of dancers and musicians. The dancers wore necklaces and colourful [5] ______ with feathers. The musicians played different [6] ______ on their instruments.

1 Answer the questions about the history of the guitar.

1. Where can you see the oldest instrument?

 ____

2. What did the travelling singers play hundreds of years ago?

 ____

3. When and where did people use guitars with six strings for the first time?

 ____

4. Who designed the classical guitar?

 ____

5. What's different about the sound of an electric guitar?

 ____

2 Match the descriptions to the photos. Write the numbers.

1. This instrument always had more strings than a guitar.
2. You need electricity to play this guitar.
3. This is the design of today's classical guitars.
4. It is possible that Queen Hatshepsut listened to this instrument.

3 What is your favourite musical instrument? Look for a photo of the first instrument and a photo of it today.

My favourite instrument is ______________.

People played it for the first time in ______________.

4 Answer the questions about carnival in Brazil.

1 When do they celebrate carnival?

2 How do they celebrate it?

3 What is the name of the music you can hear everywhere?

4 Why do you think this music is so popular?

5 Write about how you celebrate carnival in your country.

- Do you celebrate at home or at school?
- Do you wear a costume?
- Is there a party or a parade?

6 How did you make your musical instrument? Write about it and draw a picture.

Materials and method

1 Order the events from Rebeca's story.

a 

☐ She met the girls' football team.

b 

☐ They won an important competition.

c 

☐ The coach chose her for the girls' team.

d 

1 She played football with the boys at school.

e 

☐ She wants to travel to different countries.

f 

☐ She trained with her dad and brother.

2 Answer the questions about Rebeca.

1 Where is she from? ______________________

2 What does her mum think about football? ______________________

3 What did the boys think at first about playing with her? ______________________

____

4 How long did she train with her dad and brother? ______________________

5 Why does she want to learn to speak English? ______________________

____

3 What do you want to be really good at? How are you going to work hard at it?

____

____

Listen and write. There is one example.

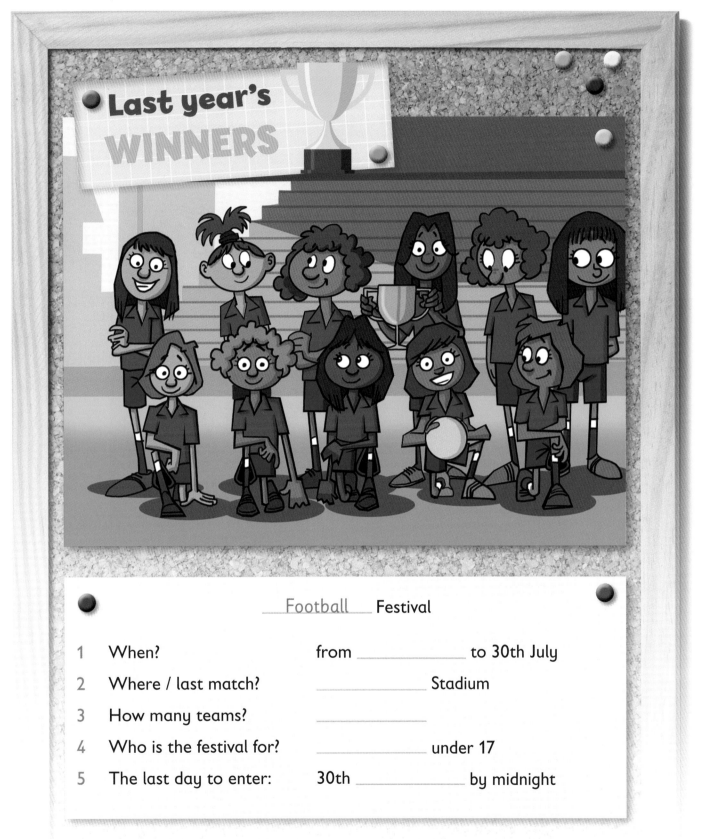

Last year's WINNERS

Football Festival

1 When? from ________ to 30th July

2 Where / last match? ________ Stadium

3 How many teams? ________

4 Who is the festival for? ________ under 17

5 The last day to enter: 30th ________ by midnight

1 4.27 **Where did Michael get each of these things? Listen and write a letter in each box. There is one example.**

[D] Volleyball

[ ] Book

[ ] Guitar

[ ] Tortoise

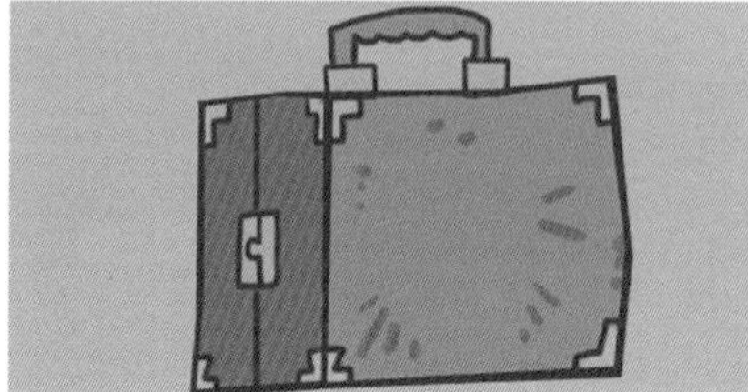

[ ] Suitcase

[ ] Ticket

A

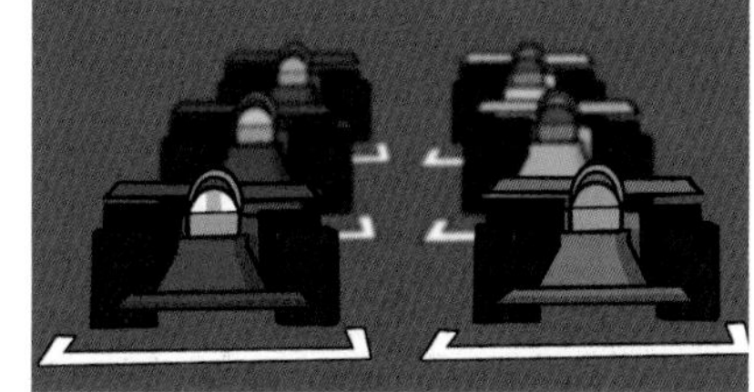

B

C

D

E

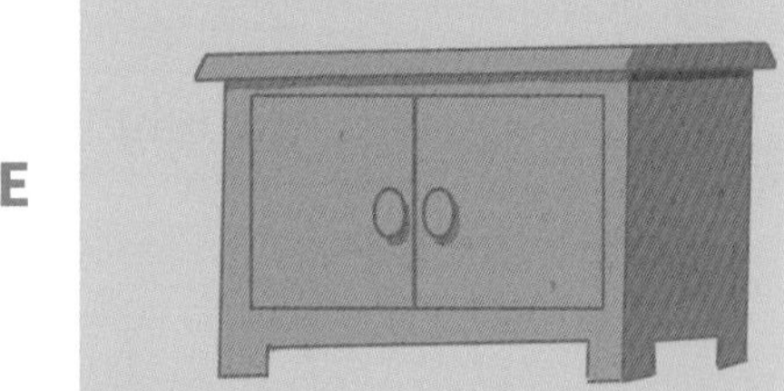

F

G

H

1 Read the instructions. Play the game.

FINISH

?

You've stopped to go to a pop concert. Go back 5 squares.

?

have

put

?

be

?

?

do

You went to bed late before the match. Go back 3 squares.

?

You've just taken your friend's queen at chess. Have another turn.

You're trying hard to win the match. Go forward 4 squares.

?

see

?

go

?

You haven't finished the crossword puzzle. Miss a turn.

1

lose

START

win

?

You've won your race. Go forward 2 squares.

INSTRUCTIONS

Roll the dice and move.

On green squares, say the word.

On ? squares, answer the question on the card.

On purple squares, say the past participle of the verb and spell it.

Review ••• Units 1–3

Have you ever played in a volleyball match?

1 Ask people in your class and write their names.

Find someone who:

_______________ has played in a volleyball match

_______________ has played chess

_______________ has won a prize

_______________ has been on a stage

_______________ has played the drums

_______________ has met a famous musician

_______________ has done a quiz

_______________ has run a race

2 What did you find out about the class?

Everyone has …

No-one has …

3 Read the email. How many questions does Katy ask? _______________

Hello!

Hi William!

How are you? Thank you so much for your email. I've just come home from school. We've had an amazing week. It's been Science week at school and we've found out lots of interesting information about the environment among other things.

Last Monday, we went to the Science Museum. We heard about wild animals like tortoises and eagles. We then explored the insect section, which was the best! We saw a lot of butterflies and beetles, but we didn't have enough time to see them all. There were too many! We might go again in January when you come and visit, if you want.

Then two days ago, on 8th September, we went to some woods near the stream. Do you remember we walked there last June? We stayed the night in a tent. I've never camped before and I forgot to take my torch. We explored some caves and found out how to make a fire with wood and stones. I couldn't do it, but someone else in my class could.

Have you been on a school trip yet this year? Please write soon and tell me about it!

Love

Katy

4 Read Katy's email again. Answer the questions.

1 Why has Katy had an amazing week? Because it's been Science week at school.
2 What did Katy find out? ______
3 Which section did Katy enjoy the most? ______
4 Did Katy see everything she wanted to see in the museum? ______
5 When might Katy go again? ______
6 Where did Katy go on 8th September? ______
7 Has William ever been there before? ______
8 What did she forget to take? ______

5 Plan a reply to Katy's email. Think about your last school trip.

- Where did you go? Look at the pictures and tick ✓.

- What date did you go? ______
- What did you see? ______
- What did you learn about? ______
- What did you like the best? ______

6 Write your email. Use your notes from Activity 5.

CHECK!
Have you answered all the questions in Activity 5?
Have you used the format of an email?
Have you used the correct vocabulary and grammar?
Is your spelling correct?

Time of our lives

My unit goals

- I want to ______________________
____
- To do this, I will ______________________
____
- I will say and write ____ new words.

My mission diary

How was it? Draw a face.

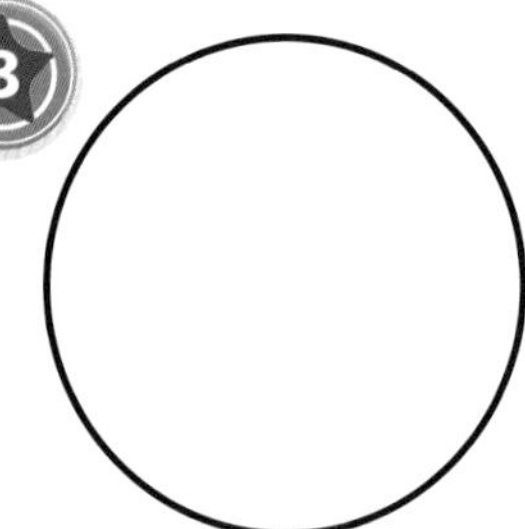

My favourite stage:

- I can talk about what was happening in the past. ☐
- I can tell the time. ☐
- I can ask and answer questions with *How long*, *for* and *since*. ☐
- I can listen for information to choose the correct answer. ☐
- I completed Level 4 Unit 4. ☐

Go to page 120 and add to your word stack!

1 Match. Write the verbs.

1	m	make	ed
	m	meet	arch
2	fe	______	fer
	fe	______	~~ake~~
3	se	______	idy
	se	______	pair
4	pre	______	ad
	pre	______	~~eet~~
5	t	______	nd
	t	______	pare
6	re	______	ry
	re	______	tch

2 Complete the sentences with the words in the box.

~~fetched~~ tidy looked after make sure repair preparing

1 Mum's just fetched Grandma from the station.
2 Last weekend my older cousin ______ me.
3 My dad's going to ______ my bike.
4 Who's ______ lunch today? I'm really hungry!
5 Michael, when are you going to ______ your bedroom?
6 Please ______ you write your names at the top of the exam paper.

Sounds and spelling

3 4.28 Listen and repeat. Circle the *ee* sound.

m(ee)t tidy lucky wheel

4 Read and write the missing words.

1 Is it safe to climb that _ _ _ _ in your garden?
2 I write in my _ _ _ _ _ every day.
3 Be quiet, please! You're very _ _ _ _ _ today!

DIVERSICUS

1 Read and answer.

1 What did the Friendly family hit on the jungle path? They hit a hole.

2 How was Mr Friendly driving? ______

3 When did the bus arrive? ______

4 What was Mrs Friendly doing on the bus? ______

5 Who's going to help Mr Friendly in the jungle? ______

6 What are Jim and Jenny going to do now? ______

2 Complete the text with the words in the box.

~~worried~~ while driving jungle pleased was path prepare

Su-Lin's Diary

Yesterday everyone was [1] worried because the Friendly family got to Diversicus late. It was time to [2] ______ lunch, but they were having an adventure in the [3] ______! While Jim and Jenny were having this adventure, we had to study for an exam. I didn't mind because I like studying, but Pablo wasn't very [4] ______.

This is what happened. They were driving along a [5] ______ in the jungle when they had a problem. Mr Friendly wasn't going fast – he was [6] ______ carefully – but he hit a hole and a tyre burst. They had to change the tyre. A bus came [7] ______ they were repairing the tyre, so they got on. On the bus, everyone [8] ______ singing and they were having a great time. When they got here, Mr Friendly went back to the jungle with Marc to fetch their home. Jim and Jenny's mum said they had to study for the exam. We're all going to do it tomorrow. No problem – I'm ready!

3 Review the story.

I think the story is **great** / **good** / **OK** / **not very good**.

My favourite character is ______.

My favourite part is when ______.

1 Read and match.

1 I was tidying my room when
2 While they were playing
3 I was looking after my little brother
4 He was preparing lunch when
5 While Mum was repairing my bike,
6 While we were walking to school,
7 I was fetching a book for my
8 They were running into the station

a Grandma phoned her.
b when the train left.
c we saw our maths teacher.
d mum when Dad called me.
e he cut his finger.
f when he fell over.
g I found my mum's bracelet.
h volleyball, it started to rain.

2  Look at the three pictures. Answer the questions about the first picture.

Think of a name for the older boy. ....

Think of a name for the younger boy. ....

Where were they? ....

Who were they with? ....

What were they doing? ....

Now write 20 or more words about the story.

....

....

....

....

1 Read and match. Write the numbers.

1 Yesterday Richard got up at five past nine.
2 He had a shower at twenty past nine.
3 He ate cereal for breakfast at quarter to ten.
4 He was going to work on the bus when he met George at ten past ten.
5 He sent Holly a message at twenty to one.
6 Holly and Richard had lunch together at five to one.
7 Richard finished work at twenty-five past six.
8 At home, he prepared dinner at quarter to eight.

2 Look at the clocks and write the times.

It's twenty-five past two.

3 Write five times. Work with a friend. Say what you do at those times.

You wrote twenty to eight. What do you do at that time?

I have breakfast at twenty to eight.

1 Complete the sentences with *for* or *since*.

1 She's lived here ___for___ six months.
2 I haven't been to school ______ 21st June.
3 We've studied English ______ four years.
4 I've known my teacher ______ September.
5 She hasn't seen me ______ Monday.
6 I've had this book ______ four months.
7 They've stayed in that hotel ______ two days.
8 Mrs Black has taught this class ______ 15th January.
9 He's been in that classroom ______ twenty-five past three.

2 Complete the interview with the questions in the box.

~~Are you married?~~ Have you ever been to New York?
Have you played at many festivals? How long have you had that guitar?
How long have you lived in London? How long have you played the guitar?
Have you studied the guitar? How long have you been married?

Interview with BRUNO JUPITER

Yesterday I spoke to Bruno Jupiter about his life as a musician. First, a personal question, Bruno.

1 Are you married?
Yes, I am. My wife's name is Sarah.

2 ______
I've been married for five years.

3 ______
No, I haven't. I've never studied the guitar with a teacher. I taught myself.

4 ______
I've played it since I was a boy.

5 ______
This is my favourite guitar. I've had it since I was 18.

6 ______
Yes, lots – in many different countries!

7 ______
Yes, I have. I've stayed in New York twice.

8 ______
I've lived in London for three years.

1 Label the map with the words in the box.

~~a line of longitude~~ a line of latitude the equator the Greenwich Meridian

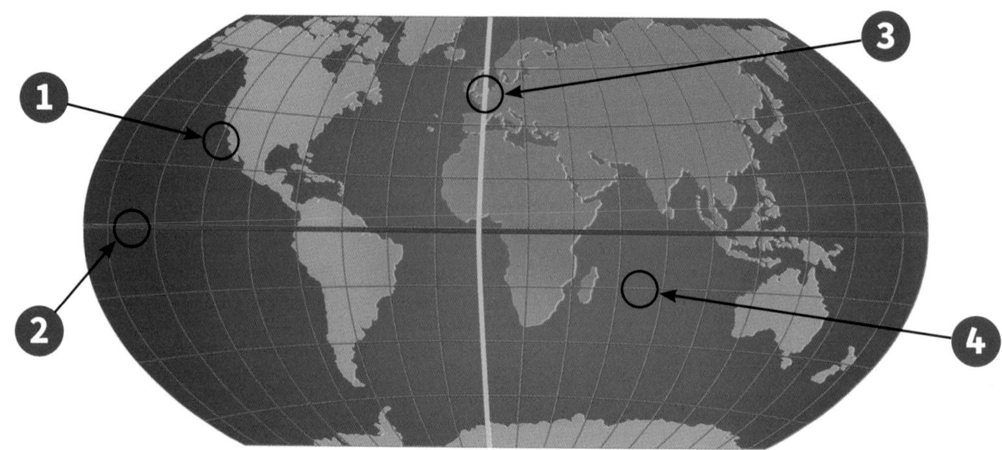

1 a line of longitude
3
2
4

2 Match to make sentences.

1 Lines of longitude — c
2 Lines of latitude
3 The Greenwich Meridian
4 Some larger countries
5 Different countries are

a in different time zones.
b go around Earth.
c go up and down Earth.
d passes through London.
e have three or more time zones.

3 Imagine that it is 8.00 in the morning. Answer the questions.

1 You're at home. What are you doing? ____________
2 What time is it now in London? ____________
3 What do you think children are doing there? ____________

4 Find out which countries the Greenwich Meridian passes through. Use the internet to help you.

____

____

5 How do you celebrate New Year's Eve in your country?

Do you eat any special food? What is it?

____

Are there any special traditions like putting an onion on your door?

____

6 Complete the fact file about Colombia. Use the internet to help you.

Name: Colombia

Continent: ______________

Capital city: ______________

Language: ______________

Time zone: ______________

Size: ______________ square kilometres

Number of inhabitants: ______________

Borders with:

Peru, ______________________________

Oceans/Seas:

____

Mountains:

____

1 Look at the story and the pictures to complete the sentences.

1 We know Mother Mountain lives in the forest because she wears ______________________________

____.

2 Mother Mountain looks after the forest, so the animals know ______________________________

____.

3 We think the bear seemed to be saying 'Thank you, Mother Mountain' because ______

____.

4 The men promised never to cut down trees or hurt animals because ______________

____.

2 Work with a friend. Complete the paragraph about another Mother Mountain legend. Use the picture to help you.

A few minutes later, a woman came to a river in the forest. She had a big bag of rubbish. She lifted up the bag and threw it into the river. ______________________

____

____

____

Listen and colour and write. There is one example.

1 4.30 Listen and tick (✓) the box. There is one example.

What was Katy's first job?

 A ☐   B ☐  C ✓

1 What doesn't she like about her job now?

 A ☐  B ☐  C ☐

2 What is the easiest thing about this job?

 A ☐  B ☐  C ☐

3 Which game are they going to play?

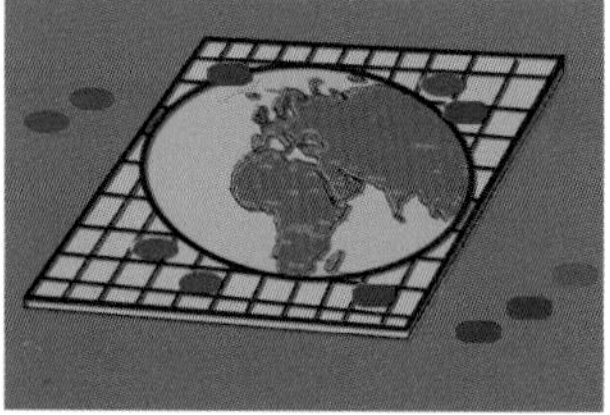 A ☐  B ☐  C ☐

4 What is Katy going to do in August?

 A ☐  B ☐  C ☐

5 How is she going to travel there?

 A ☐  B ☐  C ☐

1 Read the instructions. Play the game.

FINISH

START

INSTRUCTIONS

Roll the dice and move.

On green squares, say the word.

On orange squares, say what the people were doing.

On purple squares, say the time.

On ? squares, answer the question on the card.

Go up the ladder. Go down the rope.

Let it snow!

DIVERSICUS

My unit goals

- I want to ______________________________
  ____
- To do this, I will ______________________________
  ____
- I will say and write ____ new words.

My mission diary

How was it? Draw a face.

1 ◯ 2 ◯

3 ◯ ★ ◯

My favourite stage:

____

- I can name the seasons and different types of weather. ☐
- I can make offers to help people. ☐
- I can talk about why something happens. ☐
- I can ask and answer questions to find out information. ☐
- I completed Level 4 Unit 5. ☐

Go to page 120 and add to your word stack!

1 Read the sentences. Complete the crossword.

Across (→)

3 When water is at a temperature of 0°C, it changes into …
4 This is the season before winter.
6 This is the season after winter.
7 When clouds are very low and you can't see much, there's …
8 This is the opposite of cool.

Down (↓)

1 This is the coldest season.
2 This is the hottest season.
5 There was a lot of fog. It was very …
6 When there's a … with a lot of wind and rain, the sea is very dangerous.

1 WINTER

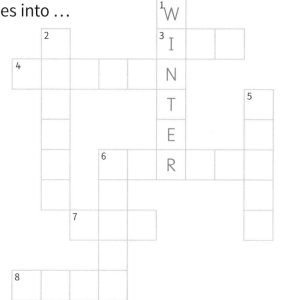

2 In each group, join three words from a word family with a line.

1

spring	fetch	bring
send	early	repair
autumn	winter	summer

2

festival	Thursday	Wednesday
January	Monday	concert
Friday	tune	Saturday

3

quarter	warm	fog
foggy	late	ice
sunny	beetle	storm

4

February	December	March
bottle	can	April
May	might	bowl

Sounds and spelling

3 4.31 Listen and repeat. Underline the stressed syllable in each word.

summer winter November winner calendar passenger doctor

4 Think of other words that end with these letters and follow the same stress patterns.

DIVERSICUS

1 Read and write *yes* or *no*.

1 Rose has given the children a group project to do. no
2 Jenny and Pablo have chosen the easiest ones. ________
3 They've got wifi. ________
4 There's an excellent bookshop in the museum. ________
5 Su-Lin will find out about the environment. ________
6 Ivan says he can eat more than a kangaroo. ________

2 Read the text. Choose the right words and write them on the lines.

Pablo's Diary

OK, I wasn't very nice yesterday, but I [1] won't be unkind again. Yesterday morning, Dad gave us a project on animals [2] ________ Patagonia. Jenny and I used the photos and video which we took [3] ________ we were on the ship, but Jim and Su-Lin had to use books because we haven't got wifi. I laughed at Jim about using books. (Not my best moment …)

Su-Lin had a great idea about going to the End of the World Museum. Jenny and I thought we [4] ________ go, but Su-Lin was really kind and asked [5] ________ to go too!

In the end, Jenny and I helped Jim and Su-Lin and we had time to go for a nice lunch. It was a great day out – and I was so horrible in the morning! I'll never [6] ________ at my friends' problems again.

1	won't	isn't	didn't	4	haven't	weren't	couldn't
2	for	on	in	5	us	we	our
3	who	when	where	6	laughed	laugh	laughing

3 Review the story.

I think the story is **great** / **good** / **OK** / **not very good**.

My favourite character is ________.

My favourite part is when ________.

1 Put the words in order. Write the sentences.

1 worry Mum, I'll / Don't / after lunch. / tidy my bedroom

Don't worry Mum, I'll tidy my bedroom after lunch.

2 morning, please? / my bike this / you repair / Dad, will

3 we get back / lunch when / We'll prepare / from town.

4 I'll / blanket for / you, Grandma. / fetch a

5 message today because / send us a / he's lost his phone. / He won't

6 the museum. / They'll / square behind / meet us in the

7 after my dog / Who'll look / the shop? / while I go into

8 late for / I hope we / the film. / won't be

2 Complete the conversations with the sentences in the box.

I'll give him some water. I'll call the doctor.
I'm not sure. I'll text him. I'll make you a snack.

1
The dog's thirsty.
I'll
2
I'm very hungry!
3
He's got a temperature.
4
When's Dad coming?

1 Order the letters. Complete the puzzle.

1 womanns
2 solablnw
3 cpkteo
4 retwin
5 ownrabdos
6 vgleo
7 maunut
8 mursem
9 dpon
10 giksin
11 gripsn
12 gedsel

				1	S	N	O	W	M	A	N

What's the secret word? ______

2 Look and read. Choose the correct words and write them on the lines. There is one example.

snowmen a sledge foggy skiing gloves summer snowballs pockets a snowboard a pond a storm autumn

This sport may sometimes be dangerous because it's fast. You go down a mountain with snow. skiing

1 This season is the hottest and sunniest. ______
2 We make these outside. They have a big body and a head. ______
3 We wear these on our hands to keep them warm. ______
4 We've got these on our clothes. We put things in them. ______
5 When there's a lot of snow, we can sit on this to go down a hill fast. ______
6 This is like a lake, but smaller. We can sometimes find one in a park. ______
7 This is like a skateboard, but it hasn't got wheels. We don't use it in hot, sunny places. ______
8 This is the weather when it's difficult to see. ______

1 Read and colour.

brown	grey	blue
They took their umbrellas	He studied hard at school,	I haven't got any gloves,

pink	black	purple
It started snowing this morning,	I'll prepare lunch	We're going to walk across the desert,

so he did well in his exams.	because we're all hungry.	because it was raining.
so we'll go sledging this afternoon.	so we'll need strong boots and water.	so I'll put my hands in my pockets.

2 Complete the sentences with *so* or *because*. Use a comma with *so*.

1 It was very hot , so I went for a swim.
2 I made a snowman ________ there was a lot of snow.
3 I'll be ten minutes late ________ I didn't catch the 8.15 bus.
4 My parents went out ________ Grandma looked after me.
5 My chair's broken ________ we'll repair it this afternoon.
6 We're going ice skating ________ there's ice on the pond.

1 Label the diagram with the words in the box.

~~axis~~ equator North Pole South Pole northern hemisphere southern hemisphere

1 axis
2 ______
3 ______
4 ______
5 ______
6 ______

2 Complete the text with the words in the box.

~~summer~~ sun winter lower higher South

It's [1] summer in the **northern** hemisphere when the North Pole tilts towards the [2] ______. This means that the temperatures are [3] ______. At the same time, it's [4] ______ in the **southern** hemisphere because the [5] ______ Pole is tilting away from the sun. This means the temperatures are [6] ______.

3 Read about the northern hemisphere and write the seasons.

1 Spring begins in March. The temperature gets higher and there is sometimes a lot of rain. Flowers start to grow on plants and many animals have babies in spring.

2 ______ begins in December. The temperature is low and it may snow. Some trees lose their leaves.

3 ______ begins in June. The temperature is high and there is less rain in some places. Lots of fruit is ready to eat.

4 ______ begins in September. It begins to get colder and there is more rain. The leaves on some trees start to change colour.

4 Correct the sentences about the seasons in Argentina.

1 Summer begins in June and winter begins in December in Argentina.

Winter begins

2 It is hot all year in the south of Argentina.

3 You can only see penguins in Argentina in winter.

4 You can only swim in the sea in summer.

5 Complete the graph with the average temperature for each month where you live. Use the internet to help you.

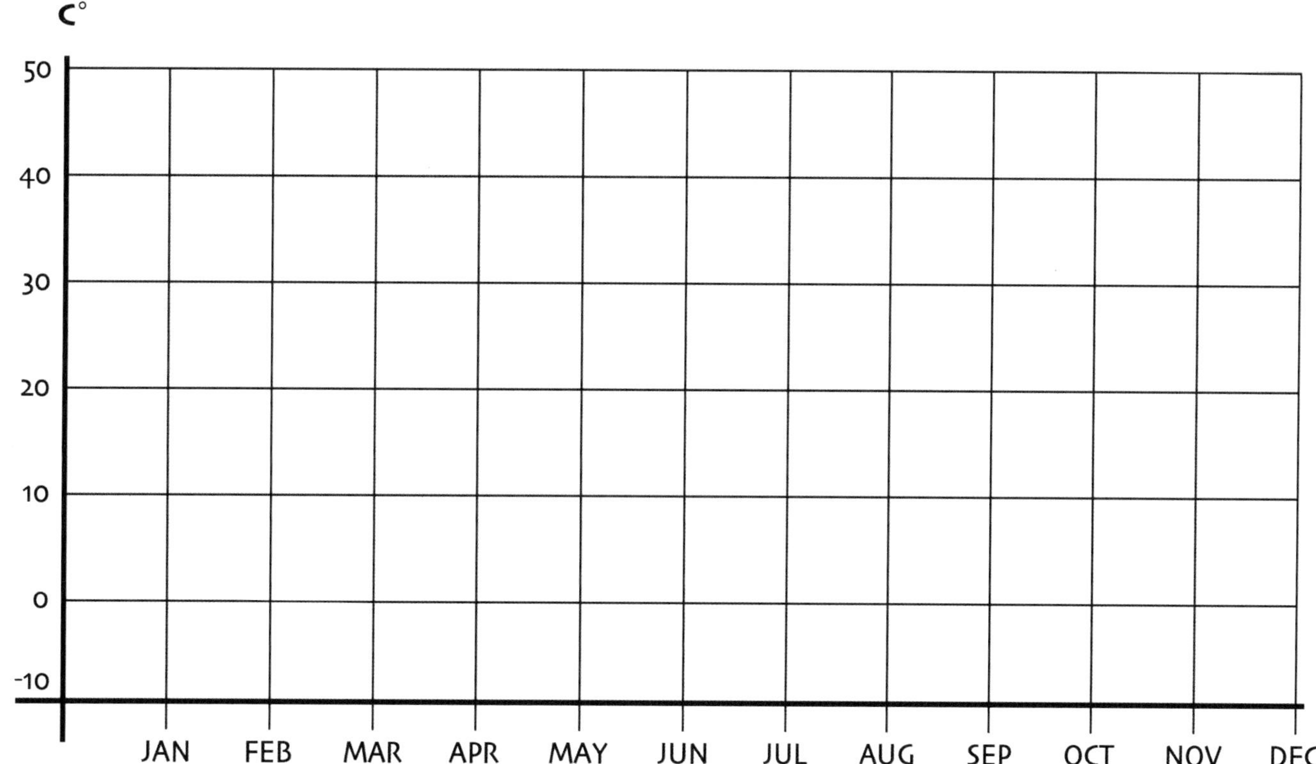

6 Look at your graph in Activity 5 and answer the questions.

1 Which months are the hottest?

2 Which months are the coldest?

1 Complete the sentences about *Tomás and the snowman*.

1 Tomás and Valentín were from Patagonia, in Argentina.
2 Valentín was ______ years old.
3 Valentín knocked the snowman down because ______.
4 Tomás was sad because ______.
5 Valentín said sorry to Tomás and promised to make ______.

2 Are these sentences true or false? Correct the false sentences.

1 Tomás was older than Valentín. False: Tomás was ______
2 The hill where the brothers played was in front of their house. ______
3 Valentín liked snowboarding. ______
4 The boys used a stone to make the snowman's nose. ______
5 Tomás and Valentín made more snowmen later that day. ______

3 Read the questions. Then discuss your answers with a partner.

1 Valentín knocked El Viejo down. Did he do the right thing or the wrong thing?
2 Have you ever made a member of your family sad? Why? What did you do?

Listen and tick (✓) the box. There is one example.

1 What was Dad's favourite activity in the snow?

 A ☐

 B ☑

 C ☐

2 Which is Valentín's favourite season?

 A ☐

 B ☐

 C ☐

3 Which boots are Valentín's?

 A ☐

 B ☐

 C ☐

4 What have the boys forgotten to pack?

 A ☐

 B ☐

 C ☐

5 What do the boys take to eat and drink?

 A ☐

 B ☐

 C ☐

6 What time did Mum tell the boys to come home?

 A ☐

 B ☐

 C ☐

1 4.33 **Look at the notes about Harry's new DVD. Listen and make sentences to answer the questions.**

Harry's new DVD

What about	Spring animals
How long / DVD	70 minutes
Who / from	Grandma
Got / music	Yes
Like best	Butterflies

2 4.34 **Now ask questions about Sarah's new DVD. You will hear each answer, but you don't need to write in the Speaking exam.**

Sarah's new DVD

What about	?
How long / DVD	?
Who / from	?
Got / music	?
Like best	?

1 Read the instructions. Play the game.

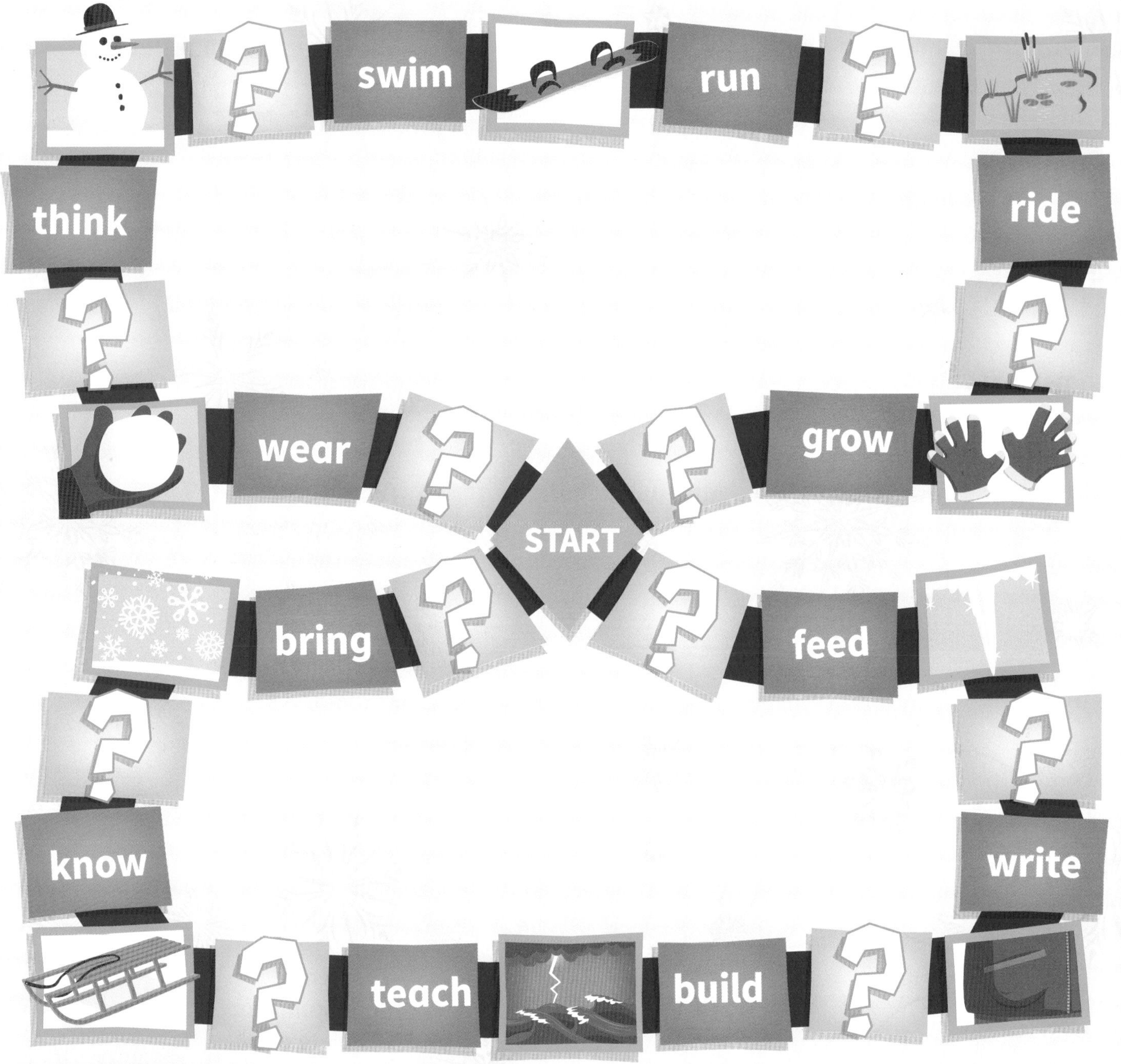

swim

run

ride

think

wear

grow

START

bring

feed

know

write

teach

build

INSTRUCTIONS

Choose four pictures. Write the words in your notebook. You must collect these.

Roll the dice and move.

Collect your four words. Tick ✓ them in your notebook.

On green squares, say the word.

On ? squares, answer the question on the card.

On orange squares, say the past participle of the verb and spell it.

6 Working together

DIVERSICUS

My unit goals

- I want to ______________________________
- To do this, I will ______________________________
- I will say and write ____ new words.

My mission diary

How was it? Draw a face.

My favourite stage:

____

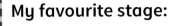

I can names jobs and places of work. ☐

I can use tag questions to check that a statement is true. ☐

I can use short questions to show interest and surprise. ☐

I can read, understand and complete a factual text. ☐

I completed Level 4 Unit 6. ☐

Go to page 12 and add to you word stack!

1 Look and write the jobs. Find the words in the wordsearch and check your spelling.

A	Q	W	P	I	L	O	T	N	O	Y	S	C
L	P	H	O	T	O	G	R	A	P	H	E	R
H	T	L	L	Z	P	X	E	T	Y	H	N	J
B	U	S	I	N	E	S	S	M	A	N	G	P
B	M	F	C	U	Z	O	A	E	C	X	I	R
V	A	M	E	K	I	E	G	C	T	K	N	O
Q	N	N	O	A	A	Y	U	H	Y	P	E	Y
C	A	X	F	B	C	U	T	A	H	K	E	O
O	G	W	F	T	E	N	K	N	S	U	R	P
O	E	Y	I	U	R	W	A	I	T	E	R	K
K	R	E	C	Y	S	G	U	C	N	O	T	L
W	C	S	E	N	W	I	S	T	B	R	T	I
A	F	I	R	E	F	I	G	H	T	E	R	K

1 

manager

2 

3

4 

5 

6 

7 

8 

9 

10 

2 Circle the different word.

1 pilot (drum) airport journey
2 manager office desk cushion
3 pop star tune stage uniform
4 stream mechanic taxi lorry
5 firefighter building brave corner
6 cave pond businesswoman stone
7 ambulance hospital nurse storm
8 waiter airport cook restaurant

Sounds and spelling

3 4.35 Listen and repeat. Underline the stressed word in each compound noun.

<u>film</u> star bus stop pop star post office train station

4 4.36 Listen and repeat.

The pop star's playing rock music at the train station.
The police officer and the film star are at the post office.

1 4.37 Read and write *yes* or *no*. Listen and check.

1 They aren't in Australia, are they? ___no___
2 They invented K-pop music in South Korea, didn't they? ______
3 Jim and Jenny's dad's got a robot in the kitchen, hasn't he? ______
4 Robots don't always look like people, do they? ______
5 They're designing robot teachers, aren't they? ______
6 The robot which Mrs Friendly's looking at isn't playing the guitar, is it? ______
7 Ivan hasn't bought a kitten, has he? ______
8 Ivan's puppy can walk, can't it? ______

2 Complete the text with the words in the box.

~~South~~ strong violin robots friendliest looking kitchen Yesterday

Jim's Diary

We're in [1] ___South___ Korea at the moment and we've seen some of the robots which they make. Sometimes people don't think about it, but there are lots of different kinds of [2] ______ and they can do lots of different things. People use them in the [3] ______, and to clean floors, and they're also very important for work. [4] ______ afternoon, we went to a place where they had some really interesting robots. There was one which could play the [5] ______, which my mum liked, and another one which could lift cars. Su-Lin said it was as [6] ______ as Ivan! I think the [7] ______ robot was a puppy, and so did Ivan! While we were [8] ______ at one of the biggest robots in the world, Ivan bought a robot puppy. His name's Mr Barker. We couldn't believe it when Ivan came out of the building with Mr Barker!

3 Review the story.

I think the story is **great** / **good** / **OK** / **not very good**.
My favourite character is ______.
My favourite part is when ______.

1 Read and match.

1 He isn't repairing the bicycle,
2 Your grandparents are looking after your little brother,
3 She made sure it was the right answer,
4 We didn't send any messages,
5 You've met my cousin,
6 She's going to prepare a snack,
7 You can tidy the kitchen,
8 You haven't fetched the shopping from the car,

a did we?
b have you?
c isn't she?
d can't you?
e aren't they?
f didn't she?
g is he?
h haven't you?

2  Listen and draw lines. There is one example.

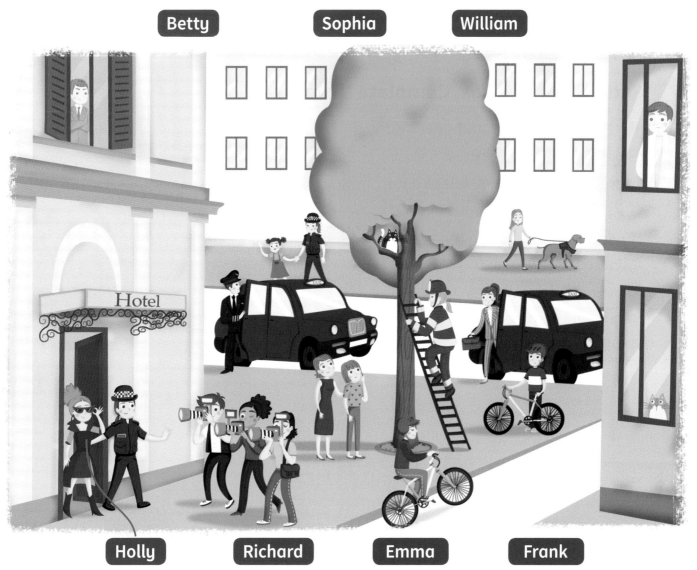

Betty Sophia William

Hotel

Holly Richard Emma Frank

1 Write the words in the correct picture.

~~office~~ ~~helmet~~ ~~businesswoman~~ ~~phone~~ police station gloves fire station cupboard boots manager desk engineer factory mechanic computer pocket

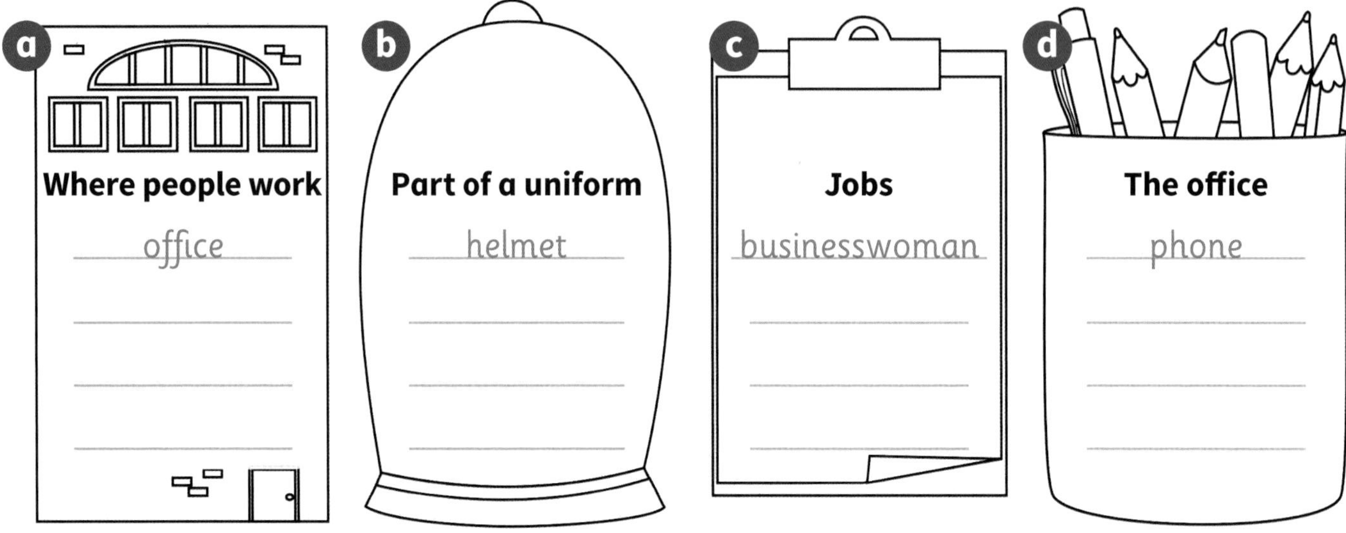

2 Read the sentences. Complete the puzzle.

1 At half past nine, the managers went to a big office to have a …

2 There are lots of desks, telephones and computers in this place of work.

3 My dad watches this on the television. It tells him about things that are happening in the world.

4 Buying and selling things is sometimes called …

5 Police officers usually work at the …

6 Robots make cars in a …

7 This is someone who stops other people doing bad things.

8 This is the big lorry that firefighters use.

9 These are the special clothes people have to wear for some jobs.

1 M E E T I N G
2
3
4
5
6
7
8
9

Write a sentence using the secret word.

1 Complete the conversations with a short question.

My son works in a factory.
Does 1 ?
Her cousin's just fallen into the pond!
2 ?
They didn't have a meeting last week.
3 ?
He won't tidy his room!
4 ?

2 Helen's Uncle Robert is a mechanic and she's visiting him at work to ask him about his job. Read the conversation and write the best letter (A–H) for each of Uncle Robert's answers.

1 **Helen:** Hello, Uncle Robert. Have you just repaired that red car?
Robert: D

2 **Helen:** That's good, because I'm going to ask you more questions!
Robert: ______

3 **Helen:** Your job. What have you just done to this car behind us?
Robert: ______

4 **Helen:** Have you? Do you usually do that for people?
Robert: ______

5 **Helen:** Oh, I see! How many cars have you worked on this week?
Robert: ______

6 **Helen:** I want to be a mechanic when I grow up.
Robert: ______

A Go away! Don't ask him now.
B Haven't you? I tidied it yesterday.
C Are you? What about?
D Yes, and now I'm having a break. **(example)**
E Not always, but that one's mine!
F Do you? Well, you can start today. You can help me tidy my office.
G I've repaired about 12, I think.
H Oh, I've only washed that blue one!

1 Match the robots with the work they do.

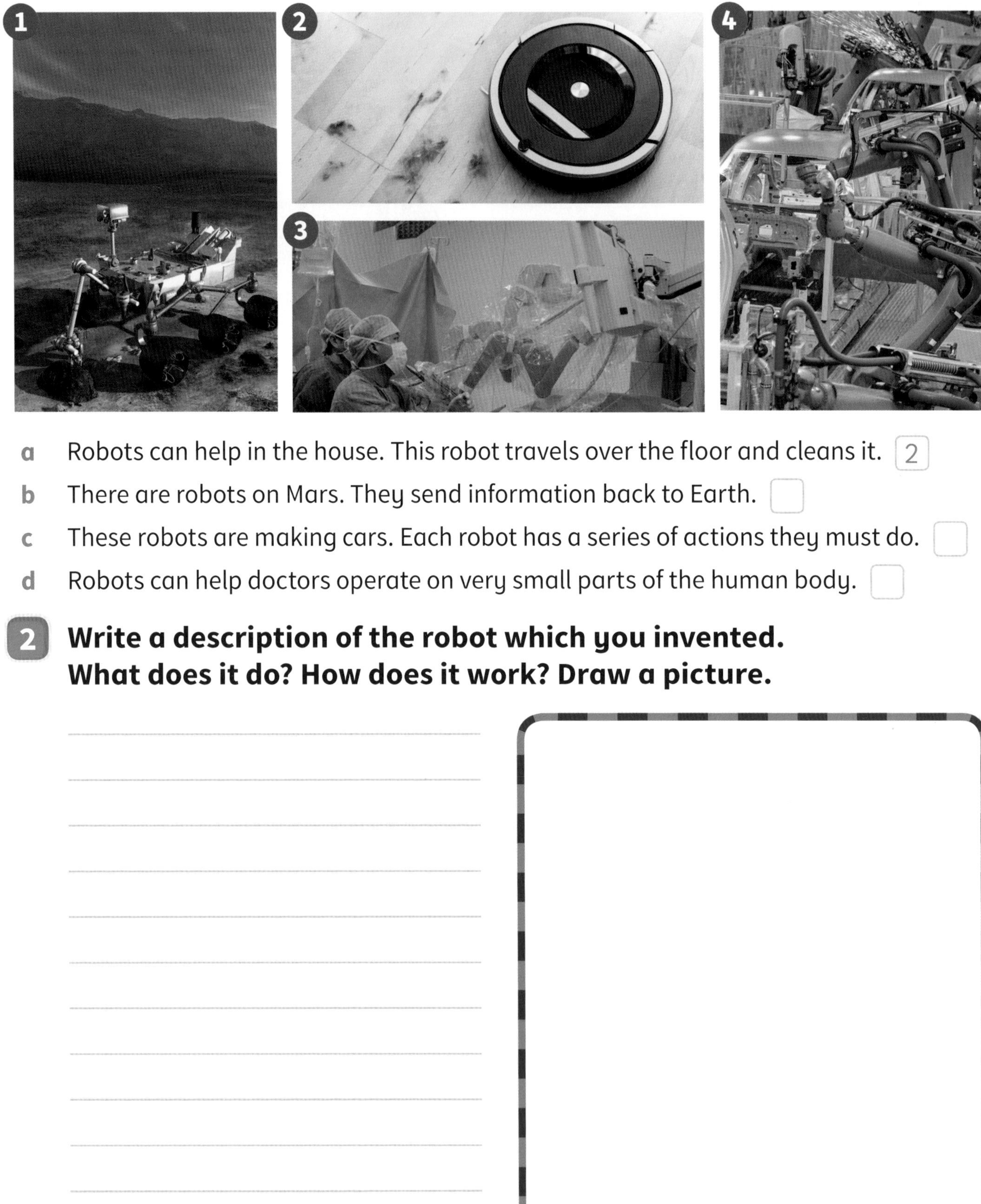

a Robots can help in the house. This robot travels over the floor and cleans it. 2

b There are robots on Mars. They send information back to Earth. ☐

c These robots are making cars. Each robot has a series of actions they must do. ☐

d Robots can help doctors operate on very small parts of the human body. ☐

2 Write a description of the robot which you invented. What does it do? How does it work? Draw a picture.

3 Complete the descriptions of South Korean inventions with the words in the box.

~~clean~~	keep	everything	money	screen	floor	music	travel

1 This helps you clean the ______ and it works with water.

2 You can do ______ you want to do by touching the ______.

3 If you use this when you ______, you don't need ______.

4 You can ______ all your ______ here.

4 Read about the kimchi fridge and answer the questions.

When you open this fridge, you won't find any of the foods you usually see in fridges. There's no milk, no cheese and no yoghurts. This fridge is only for one food – kimchi, one of the most popular foods in Korea. It's a cabbage dish which is difficult to make and very difficult to keep in good condition. Koreans eat kimchi with many different meals and with the invention of the kimchi fridge, they can enjoy it all year. A lot of Koreans say that the kimchi fridge is the most important thing in their kitchen.

1 How is this fridge unusual? ______

2 Why is it important in Korea? ______

______

3 What do you think is the most important thing in your kitchen? Why?

______

1 Match the actions in the story to their consequences.

1 The children don't like Buddie.
2 Seo-joon says he'll help Buddie.
3 Seo-joon and Buddie spend a lot of time together.
4 Buddie learns to understand children.
5 Seo-joon's maths improves and he's more friendly.

a They become good friends.
b The kids now like Seo-joon.
c All the children in the class now like Buddie.
d Buddie asks Seo-joon for help.
e Buddie offers to help Seo-joon with maths.

2 Complete the story planner for *Buddie and Seo-joon's adventure*.

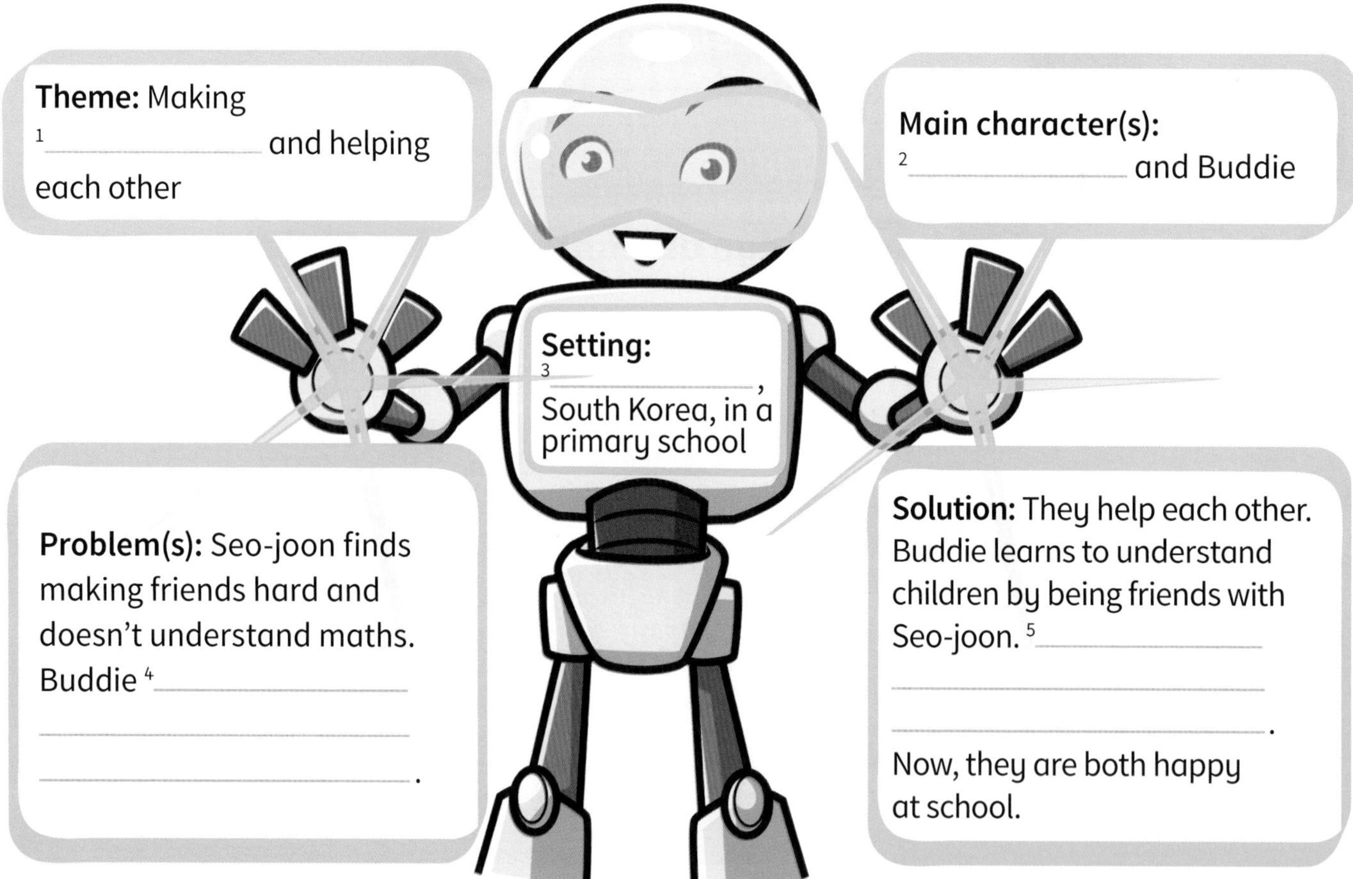

Theme: Making [1] ____________ and helping each other
Main character(s): [2] ____________ and Buddie
Setting: [3] ____________, South Korea, in a primary school
Problem(s): Seo-joon finds making friends hard and doesn't understand maths. Buddie [4] ____________ ____________ ____________.
Solution: They help each other. Buddie learns to understand children by being friends with Seo-joon. [5] ____________ ____________ ____________. Now, they are both happy at school.

3 Read the questions. Then discuss your answers with a partner.

1 Do you think the principal sent Buddie back to the factory? How do you know? Do you think he made the right decision?

2 Why do you think Buddie took the children outside to study maths? How was the lesson going to be different?

Find the differences and make sentences in pairs.

A

B

1 Read the text. Choose the right words and write them on the lines.

Journalists

Example Some people might think that being a journalist is an easy job,
1 but actually it is quite ________ to become a famous journalist. Many
2 journalists ________ been to university and they know how to
3 write about different subjects, ________ celebrities, sports or cooking.
4 Journalists often have to ________ to meetings with their manager to talk about changes in the newspaper. Many journalists work
5 ________ a photographer and they enjoy being out of the office.
6 Journalists ________ have to wear a uniform, but they usually have a laptop and a phone. If there is a very important story, they
7 ________ work for more than 12 hours a day. It's a busy job.
8 If you want to be a journalist, a ________ way to start is to write
9 something for a school newspaper or magazine. Later, you can ________ if you want to work on TV or on the radio, or perhaps your wish is to be
10 ________ online journalist? That's a very popular kind of job for journalists now.

Example think thought thinking

1	harder	hard	hardest	6	can't	don't	mustn't
2	has	having	have	7	might	shall	need
3	like	from	for	8	better	worse	good
4	went	gone	go	9	deciding	decide	decided
5	with	by	of	10	a	one	an

1 Read the instructions. Play the game.

START
You played in the park in a storm. Miss a turn.
eat
buy
make
drink
It was foggy, so the school bus was late. Go back 3 squares.
You helped a police officer. Have another turn.
You helped a firefighter save a cat. Go forward 2 squares.
take
hear
You were late for school because you didn't prepare your uniform. Go back 5 squares.
drive
FINISH
send
You won first prize in the newspaper competition. Go forward 4 squares.
POLICE

INSTRUCTIONS

Roll the dice and move.

On green squares, say the word.

On ? squares, answer the question on the card.

On purple squares, say the past participle of the verb and spell it.

Review ••• Units 4–6

1 **Work with a partner. Student A chooses a person. Student B asks questions to find out who it is.**

Ben Sophia Holly Harry Emma Frank

Were you snowboarding at 9.05?

No, I wasn't.

Were you …

2 **Read the forum posts on Harry's blog. Circle the correct words.**

Everyone likes **the same** / **a different** season.

Harry's blog

Today's question: What's your favourite season?

Hi! Today I'm writing about favourite seasons. I love spring! Last year we went camping in spring. Camping is great fun, isn't it? We were preparing lunch by the tent and it was warm and sunny, but then there was a big storm ! The weather can change very quickly in spring. I'll make sure I take an umbrella this year! What's your favourite season?

KatyM

Hi Harry! I love winter as there's a lot of snow. Meeting your friends to make snowmen is the best, isn't it? I think I'll go snowboarding this year because my friend Holly was talking about it last winter!

Betty09

Hello! My favourite season's autumn . One day last year I was looking after my sister. It was warm and sunny, so we repaired our bikes and went to the river. We were swimming when it started to rain! I love swimming in the rain, don't you?

RichardD

Hi! Summer's the best! My family's just moved to the beach. Lucky, aren't we? Yesterday, I was swimming in the sea all day because it was very hot. I'll go again tomorrow with my new friends, I think!

3 Read the forum posts again. Complete the sentences with the correct online name.

1 KatyM will go snowboarding.
2 ______ thinks summer is the best.
3 ______ was making lunch outside.
4 ______ has just moved to a new house.
5 ______ loves swimming in the rain.
6 ______ talks about trying a new sport.
7 ______ went camping last year.
8 ______ enjoys the snow in winter.
9 ______ repaired two bikes.
10 ______ will take an umbrella.

4 Plan a forum post for Harry's blog.

- What's your favourite season?

 ☐  ☐  ☐  ☐

- What is the weather like in this season? ______
- What do you like doing? ______
- Where did you go last year? ______
- What will you do differently this year? ______

5 Write your forum post for Harry's blog. Use your notes from Activity 4.

CHECK!
Have you answered all the questions in Activity 4?
Have you used the format of a forum post?
Have you used the correct vocabulary and grammar?
Is your spelling correct?

7 Then and now

My unit goals

- I want to ______________________________

  ____
- To do this, I will ______________________________

  ____
- I will say and write ____ new words.

My mission diary

How was it? Draw a face.

1

2

3

★

My favourite stage:

____

I can name things in the home. ☐

I can describe objects. ☐

I can say what things are used for. ☐

I can read a story and answer questions. ☐

I completed Level 4 Unit 7. ☐

Go to page 12(and add to you word stack!

1 Order the letters and complete the crossword.

Across (→)

3 hoposam
5 heenopetl
7 surbh
8 yek
9 gridef

Down (↓)

1 ateg
2 nevo
3 paso
4 bomc
5 loitte
6 hefls

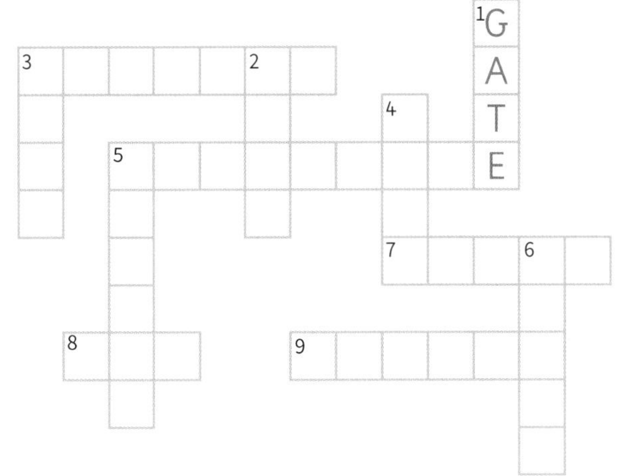

2 Match. Write the words.

1 ga gate ey
ga garden wel

2 sh ______ ap
sh ______ en

3 k ______ ampoo
k ______ ~~rden~~

4 to ______ uth
to ______ elf

5 so ______ ~~te~~
so ______ ilet

6 ov ______ ing
ov ______ er

Sounds and spelling

3 4.39 Listen and repeat. Circle the spelling of the *j* sound in each word.

fri(dge) engineer stage journey

4 Complete the words with the letters.

banda*ge* ______ sle ______ passen ______ r ______ ography
fire en ______ ne py ______ amas

1 Read and write *yes* or *no*.

1 Ivan's flown to meet the Friendly family. ___no___

2 He's borrowed Marc's car for four days. ______

3 Ivan would like to ride on a camel before he sees the old city. ______

4 Jenny's just fallen off a horse. ______

5 Jenny's broken her leg. ______

6 Jenny's cut her knee. ______

7 Jenny and Jim have forgotten their camera. ______

8 They've left their camera on the train. ______

2 Complete the text with the words in the box.

~~has~~ hurt lying because high just driven wait gone

Jenny's Diary

Today [1] ___has___ taught me that, in the future, I'll do what grown-ups ask me to do. Jim and I have [2] ______ finished having lunch with Ivan, Mum and Dad. They've [3] ______ to look around the old city, but I can't walk around because I've [4] ______ my leg. Ivan's [5] ______ from Cairo to spend time with us and he wanted to ride a camel with Jim and me.

When we got there, the camels were [6] ______ quietly on the sand and Ivan asked us to [7] ______ near them. While he was busy paying the man, I decided to get on a camel. They're very tall and I was very lucky [8] ______ it didn't stand up ... and then I fell off! It wasn't very [9] ______, but I fell onto some rocks and cut my knee quite badly. Next time, I'll listen to instructions more carefully!

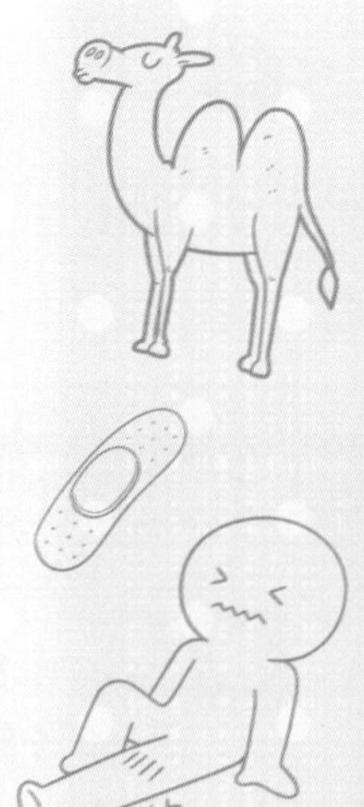

3 Review the story.

I think the story is **great** / **good** / **OK** / **not very good**.

My favourite character is ______.

My favourite part is when ______.

1 Circle eight more past participles in the wordsnake.

2 Complete the puzzle with the past participles of the verbs.

choose, chose, …
drive, drove, …
break, broke, …
leave, left, …
fly, flew, …

				1	H	U	R	T		
		2		O		N				
	3		T			D				
				4		E				
				5		R		V		
		6				S				
7						T				
			8			O				
			9		L	O				
			10			D				

hurt, hurt, …
find, found, …
forget, forgot, …
stand, stood, …
ride, rode, …

3 Complete the sentences with the past participles of the verbs.

1 Michael's just ___swum___ (swim) 200 metres butterfly in under two minutes. He's just won another Olympic gold medal!

2 Why are you tired? You've just ______ (sleep) for two hours on the sofa!

3 My little cousin's ______ (lose) his favourite teddy. We can't find it anywhere.

4 Grandpa and Dad have been at the lake for four hours, but they haven't ______ (catch) any fish yet.

5 We're drawing lots of pictures. They're going to be presents. I've ______ (draw) one for my friend and one for my mum.

6 Holly's already ______ (read) 200 pages of her new book, but she hasn't finished it yet. It's very long!

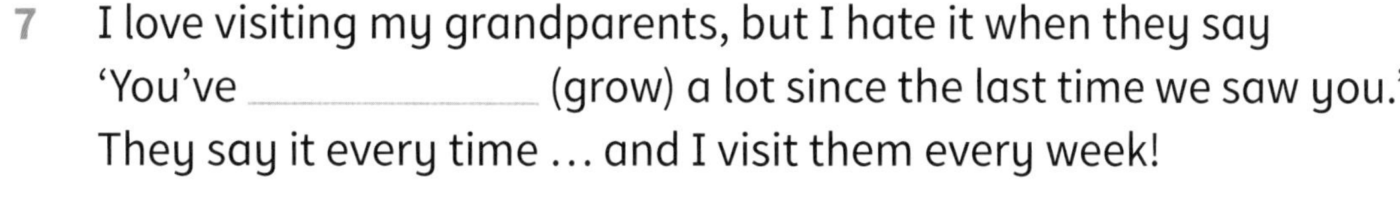

7 I love visiting my grandparents, but I hate it when they say 'You've ______ (grow) a lot since the last time we saw you.' They say it every time … and I visit them every week!

8 Richard isn't very pleased. He's just ______ (sit) on Sarah's banana. She left it on the chair!

1 Complete the sentences with adjectives. Find them in the wordsearch and check your spelling.

U	E	X	P	E	N	S	I	V	E
N	N	F	R	G	H	U	L	B	C
T	A	U	Q	B	C	K	W	S	E
I	V	L	S	R	H	L	I	U	T
D	N	L	O	U	E	L	Z	M	H
Y	P	L	E	R	A	M	X	Z	E
L	I	G	H	T	P	L	P	R	A
Y	U	B	R	O	K	E	N	T	V
F	L	U	Q	J	R	T	I	D	Y

1 We put all our clothes in the cupboard. Dad was really pleased to see our nice, ___tidy___ bedroom.

2 Be careful! There's too much coffee in that cup, so it's too ____________ !

3 We need to repair the toilet because it's ____________ .

4 Your room's very ____________ . Please tidy it before you go out with your friends.

5 Would he like some more lemonade? His glass is ____________ .

6 She bought her camera for only 20 euros. It was really ____________ .

7 That's the most ____________ car in the world. You need a million pounds to buy it!

8 Please can you help Grandma with her suitcase? It's too ____________ for her.

9 Harry didn't go to football practice yesterday, which is very ____________ because he loves football. Perhaps he hasn't been well.

10 No, there isn't a problem with Holly's rucksack. It's ____________ enough for her to carry.

2 Circle the correct words.

1 I'm looking for something really different. That isn't unusual ***too / enough***.

2 I like this game and it's cheap ***too / enough*** for me to buy with my birthday money.

3 The shopping is ***too / enough*** heavy for this bag. It'll break.

4 I need to write my story again. It's ***too / enough*** untidy to give to the teacher.

5 That watch is beautiful, but it's ***too / enough*** expensive.

6 Is this bag light ***too / enough*** to take on the plane?

7 Put your trainers in Dad's suitcase. Yours is ***too / enough*** full.

8 Mum, do you think my bedroom is tidy ***too / enough***?

1 Read and colour.

green	orange	purple
What are scissors used for?	What's a toothbrush used for?	What are combs used for?

blue	black	yellow
What's shampoo used for?	What's soap used for?	What's a glass used for?

It's used for holding a drink.	It's used for washing your hair.	They're used for cutting paper.
It's used for cleaning your teeth.	They're used for combing your hair.	It's used for washing your hands.

2 Complete the sentences about a trip to a museum with the words in the box.

~~cooking~~ to used catching for wash

1 We saw an old oven which was used for cooking meat.
2 People used soap to ______ their clothes more than a thousand years ago.
3 There was a big stone and no-one knew what it was ______ for!
4 They said eggs were used ______ pay for things instead of money.
5 We learnt about the nets that they used for ______ fish.
6 We could use our phones ______ taking pictures outside, but not inside.

1 Are these sentences true or false? Correct the false sentences.

1 Simple machines have many moving parts.

False – simple machines have ____________________

2 Machines make our lives easier.

____

3 Complex machines have few or no moving parts.

____

4 People started to use sundials in the 14th century.

____

5 Clocks are simple machines.

____

6 A digital clock has hands.

____

2 Complete the sentences.

1 Early humans didn't hunt and work when it was ___dark___.

2 The Egyptians used the ____________ of tall buildings and the sun to tell the time.

3 People burnt ____________ to tell the time.

4 Every ____________, you could hear a bell on a 14th century mechanical clock.

5 Analogue clocks have ____________.

3 Match the clocks that show the same time.

1 

2 

3 

4 

a 

b 

c 

d 20:15

4 Look at problems 1–3. How did the Ancient Egyptians solve them? Answer the questions. Use the words in the box to help you.

built ramps levers pulled rafts brought

1 

2 

3 

1 What did they use to lift the rocks?

____

2 How did they get huge rocks to the top of the pyramid?

____

3 How did they get the rocks from a different part of the country to Giza?

____

5 Read the information about Egypt and complete the fact file.

The population of Egypt is over 80 million people. The official language is Arabic, but many people can also speak English and French. The capital city is Cairo, which has the largest population. Egypt is a very hot and dry country.

Parts of the Sahara Desert and the Libyan Desert are in Egypt. The River Nile, the longest in the world, goes through Egypt. Egypt is home to the Great Pyramid of Giza, which is one of the Seven Wonders of the World.

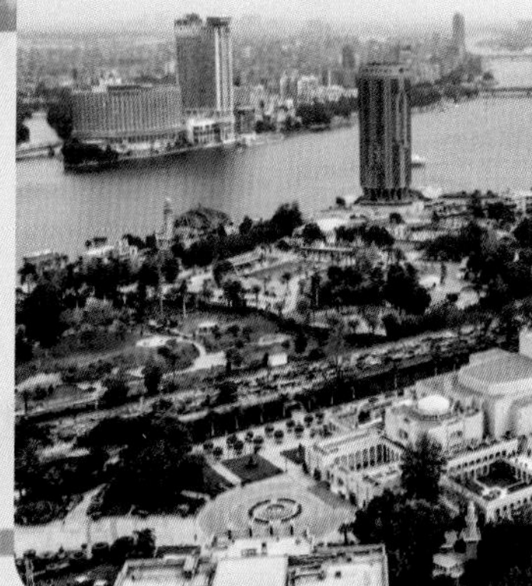

Country: ______________

Population: ______________ people

Capital: ______________

Climate: ______________ ______________

Languages: ______________, ______________, ______________

River: ______________

Most famous monument: ______________ ______________

1 Circle the correct answers.

1 When Tut became pharaoh, his life was different because he:
   - a could make changes in his country.
   - b liked having power.
   - c wasn't happy any more.

2 When Tut was ten, he:
   - a decided to control Horemheb and Ay.
   - b married a beautiful girl.
   - c got some new sandals.

3 Horemheb and Ay said Tut's new sandals:
   - a were unusual.
   - b could help him control his enemies.
   - c were for walking on hot sand.

4 Tut fell down:
   - a when he was dancing with Ank.
   - b so Horemheb threw away the sandals.
   - c and hurt his leg.

2 Look at the pictures. Why is each item important in the story? Write a sentence about each picture.

1 ______________________________

____

2 ______________________________

____

3 ______________________________

____

3 Read the questions. Then discuss with a partner.

Do you think Horemheb and Ay treated Tut fairly? Why / Why not?

Where did Emma get each of these things? Listen and write a letter in each box. There is one example.

C Bag

☐ Camel

☐ Comb

☐ Dress

☐ Rug

☐ Ring

A

B

C

D

E

F

G

H

1 **Look at the picture and read the story.**
Write some words to complete the sentences about the story.
You can use 1, 2, 3 or 4 words.

George's new rug

George hurried home from work on Thursday because his son was coming back from a trip around the world.

'It was an amazing trip, Dad!' said Frank. 'I bought you this in Dubai.' George opened the present. 'A rug! Thank you!'

'It's unusual,' said Frank, 'and it's great for the hall, isn't it?' George agreed and they put the rug on the floor.

The next morning, Frank asked 'Can I do anything to help?' George answered, 'Well, could you paint the garden gate? There's some green paint in the basement.'

After breakfast, Frank fetched the paint and went into the garden. It was a hot day and he left the door open, so their cat Betty followed him. Frank painted the back of the gate and then he went to get a drink. But sometimes Betty was naughty, so he put the paint on the shelf in the hall.

Suddenly, a big dog came into the garden. Betty ran in and jumped on the shelf because she was frightened … and the paint fell on the rug!

When George got home and saw the front of the gate, he was surprised. Then he saw the rug. 'It was Betty!' said Frank. 'And I couldn't finish the gate because we haven't got any more paint!'

Examples

George came home from work quickly on ___Thursday___ .

Frank had ___an amazing trip___ and visited lots of countries.

Questions

1 The present from Dubai was a ______________ .

2 They put it on the floor in ______________ .

3 On Friday morning, Frank wanted ______________ .

4 Frank had breakfast and then he went to get the paint from ______________ .

5 Betty went ______________ because the door was open.

6 The paint fell when the cat ______________ .

7 Frank didn't paint all of the gate because there wasn't ______________ .

1 Read the instructions. Play the game.

INSTRUCTIONS

Roll the dice and move.

On green squares, say the word.

On orange squares, say the past participle of the verb and spell it.

On ? squares, answer the question on the card.

Go up the ladder. Go down the rope.

Space travel

My unit goals

- I want to ______________________
- To do this, I will ______________________
- I will say and write ____ new words.

My mission diary

How was it? Draw a face.

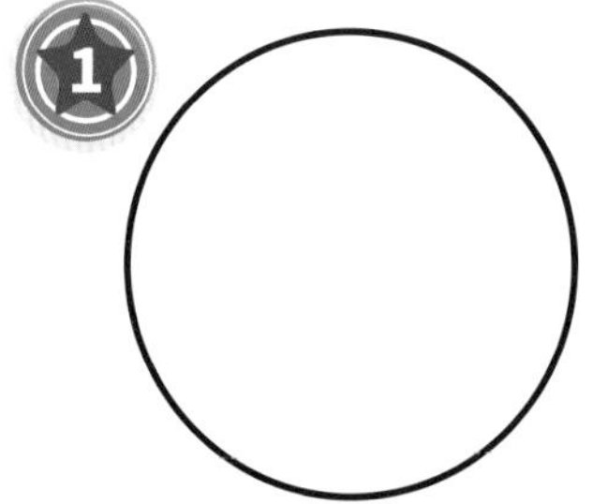

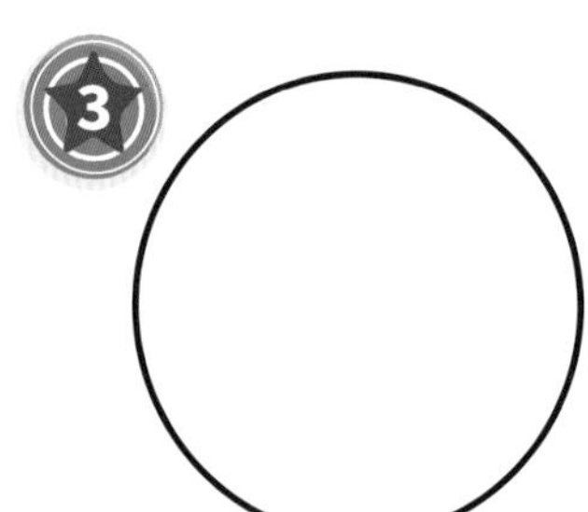

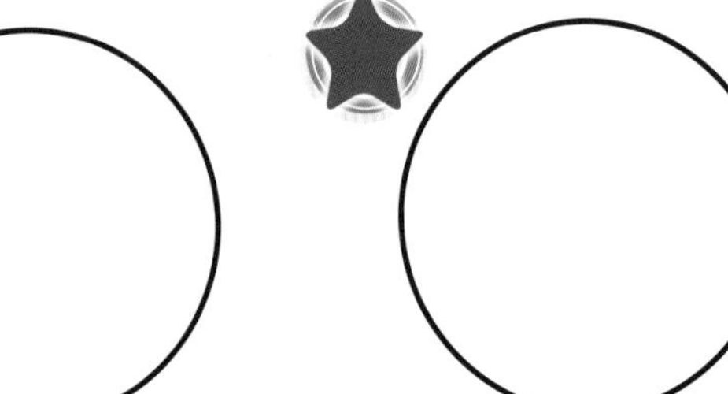

My favourite stage: ______________________

- I can talk about space travel and investigation. ☐
- I can make predictions and talk about future plans. ☐
- I can use different tenses to talk about the past. ☐
- I can read and complete a story. ☐
- I completed Level 4 Unit 8. ☐

Go to page 120 and add to your word stack!

1 Read the sentences. Complete the puzzle.

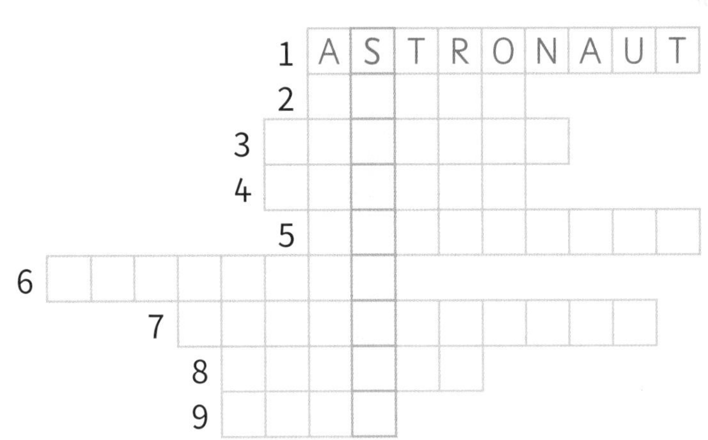

1 An … travels in space.
2 The sun, the moon, stars and planets are in …
3 Earth, Jupiter and Mars are all …
4 … is another word for spaceship.
5 We look at the stars with a …
6 … is another word for huge.
7 When something frightens you, it's …
8 An … makes a car, lorry or bus move and rockets have very big ones.
9 Pablo's astronaut is going to go into … space.

Write a sentence using the secret word.

______

______

2 Read the times. Look at the clock and write the words.

1 It's half past five. enormous
2 It's quarter past eight. ______
3 It's ten to nine. ______
4 It's ten past twelve. ______
5 It's twenty-five to ten. ______
6 It's five past eight. ______

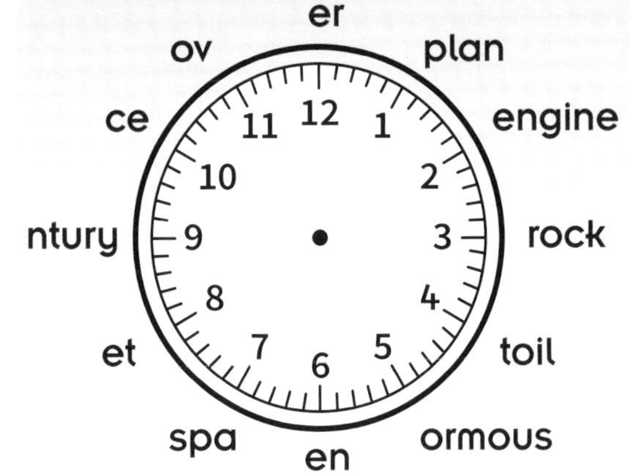

Sounds and spelling

3 4.41 Listen and repeat. Listen again and complete.

sp st sk str

1 s p ace 2 __ __ ar 3 __ __ one 4 __ __ omach 5 __ __ ip
6 __ __ __ ipe 7 __ __ ot 8 __ __ __ eam 9 __ __ i 10 __ __ __ ange

4 4.42 Listen and repeat.

Stars are special strange spots in the sky.

DIVERSICUS

1 Circle the correct words.

1 Pablo has nearly finished his **video** / **comic book**.
2 The **mechanic** / **astronaut** looks very big and strong.
3 Pablo's character is going to travel into **a deep ocean** / **deep space**.
4 Ivan thinks people **will** / **won't** eat more food.
5 The astronaut's going to use his **computer** / **oven** to get food.
6 Jim thinks we'll use planes and **trains** / **rockets** more.
7 Su-Lin thinks we'll use cars which will **sail** / **fly**.
8 Jenny thinks Pablo's comic book will be **boring** / **exciting**.

2 Read the text. Choose the right words and write them on the lines.

Pablo's Diary

This morning, we had a great conversation [1] ___about___ the future. Jim and Jenny think transport [2] ______ be different. We'll use faster and cleaner trains and planes, and people [3] ______ use their cars on roads. We also talked about my new story. It's about an astronaut [4] ______'s going to travel into deep space. He's going to be big and strong and he's going to go to new planets. He'll have a special spacesuit [5] ______ he can do amazing things. Ivan thinks that in the future, people will eat more. He didn't like the idea of using a computer to get food! That's because he's always hungry and food is very important to [6] ______.

1	for	about	to	3	won't	aren't	don't	5	so	while	if
2	is	was	will	4	which	who	what	6	his	he	him

3 Review the story.

I think the story is **great** / **good** / **OK** / **not very good**.

My favourite character is ______.

My favourite part is when ______.

1 Find and write five sentences.

~~We're going~~	feed the	repair my bicycle	past seven.
I'll	going to	at quarter	this afternoon?
Mum, are we	them tomorrow	~~Grandma~~	in a minute!
We'll meet	be any	classes next	~~tomorrow.~~
There won't	~~to visit~~	cat	week.

1 We're going to visit Grandma tomorrow.

2 ______

3 ______

4 ______

5 ______

2 Complete the conversations with the sentences in the box.

~~I'm going to drive there. I'll give you a lift.~~ Don't worry. I'll take it.
Yes. I'll make her a cake! You're right. I'll close the window.

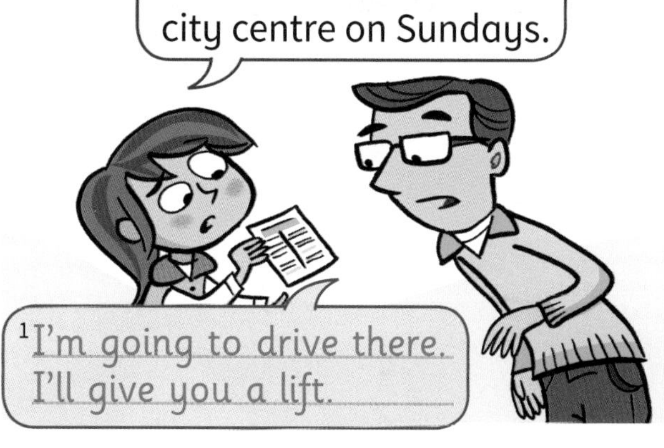

There isn't a bus to the city centre on Sundays.
1 I'm going to drive there. I'll give you a lift.

You've remembered Sarah's birthday, haven't you?
2 ______

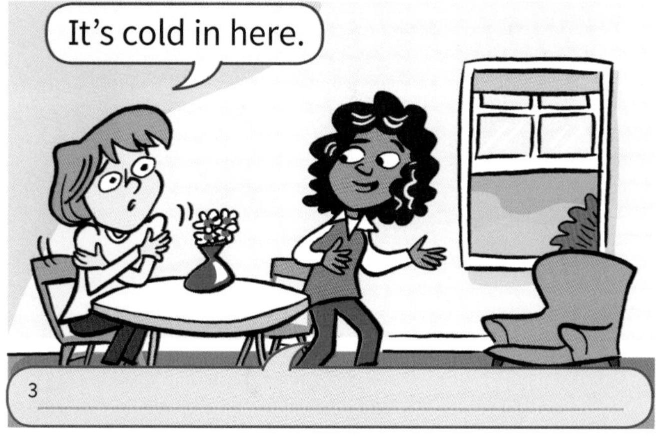

It's cold in here.
3 ______

Harry's forgotten to take his book back to the library.
4 ______

1 Read the sentences and complete the verbs.

1 I'll turn on ______ my robot dog and he can fetch the ball!
2 People will e______ deep space next century.
3 Your hand's red. Did you t______ an unusual plant?
4 We're going to s______ with Grandma in the holidays.
5 You're going to t______ the music before you start studying, aren't you?
6 Are you going to s______ any money for your holidays?
7 Please e______ the Space Museum through the door on the left.
8 We've been in the air for hours! When's the plane going to l______, Dad?

2  Read the diary and write the missing words. Write one word on each line.

I've just [1] landed on a new planet and I've put a flag into the ground. I'm [2] ______ to bring some rocks and sand back to Earth. Scientists want to find out if there's any water and if [3] ______ can live here. I think I'll [4] ______ for three days to [5] ______ the planet, but I've got [6] ______ food and drink for two weeks, so I might be here longer.

1 Oliver went to the circus last weekend. Read and put the sentences in order. Write the numbers.

a a pilot's uniform was singing beautifully on the stage when ☐

b was wearing a fantastic costume with feathers. He caught the other acrobats ☐

c was amazing. There was a strongman who was carrying three people on his ☐

d suddenly a plane landed and she climbed in! One of the acrobats ☐

e Last weekend we went to see a circus. When we entered the tent, musicians 1

f as they were flying through the air. It was the best show I've ever seen. ☐

g shoulders. He was dressed up as a firefighter. A woman who was wearing ☐

h were playing and we saw a beautiful stage with bright lights. The show ☐

2 Write questions with the past continuous and the past simple. Then invent answers.

1 What / he / do / when / his friend / arrive?

What was he doing when his friend arrived?

He was playing tennis when his friend arrived.

2 Where / they / go / when / they / meet / their teacher?

3 Where / they / explore / when / they / find / the pyramid?

4 What / she / do / when / her grandparents / arrive?

1 Read and write *Earth*, *Mars* or *Both*.

1 It's called 'the red planet'. Mars
2 The diameter of the planet is 12,742 kilometres. ______
3 It has two moons. ______
4 It has weather and seasons. ______
5 You can see a lot of water on its surface. ______
6 There are 24 hours in a day on this planet. ______

2 Read the text and answer the questions.

In August 2015, astronauts on the ISS ate the first food grown in space. Normally, plant roots always grow down into the soil where it is easy for them to take the water and nutrients. In space, because there is no gravity, the roots grow in all directions!

The plants grow in special containers. The containers have flexible walls so that the plants have space and can grow. There are bags of soil and nutrients inside the containers. Lights shine on the plants to give them the energy from light which they need.

The astronauts have grown lettuce, cabbage and tomatoes from seeds. This is very exciting news because if we can grow plants on a space station, it might be possible to grow plants on the moon and on Mars.

1 When did astronauts eat the first food grown in space? In August 2015.
2 Why do roots grow in all directions on the space station?
______
3 Why are the walls of the containers flexible?
______
4 Which three things did they grow? ______
5 Why is this news so exciting?
______

3 Circle the correct answers. Use the internet to help you.

1 Where is Italy?

a Southern Europe **b** Northern Europe
c Western Europe **d** Eastern Europe

2 What is the capital of Italy?

a Milan **b** Venice **c** Florence **d** Rome

3 How many sides of Italy are next to the sea?

a 4 **b** 3 **c** 2 **d** 1

4 What is the shape of Italy like?

a A square **b** A head **c** A hat **d** A boot

5 What is the most popular sport in Italy?

a Judo **b** Tennis **c** Football **d** Golf

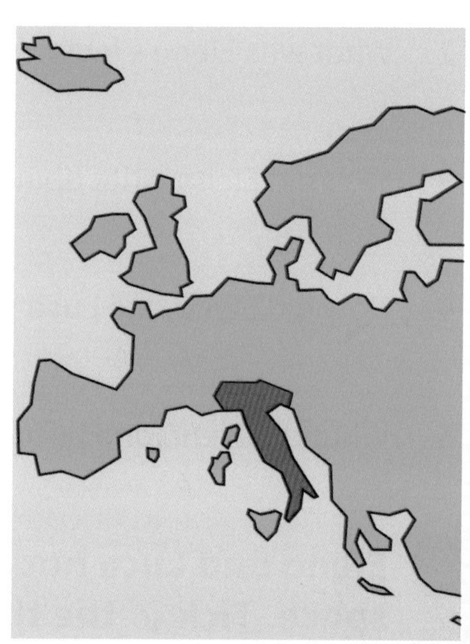

4 Complete the photo labels. Use the internet to help you.

1 ____________ is a beautiful city with many canals.

2 You can see ____________ in Rome.

3 ____________ disappeared when a volcano erupted.

4 ____________ was a famous artist who lived in Florence.

1 Answer the questions about *The Space Blog*.

1 Why did Elena and Luca go into space? They won

2 What was Elena's favourite thing about being in space?

3 Why did Elena write about food on the spaceship in Blog Post 3?

4 How did Elena and Luca feel when the engine wasn't working very well?

5 What did Elena and Luca have to do while the astronauts were fixing the engine?

2 Elena and Luca had to do lots of things before they went into space. Tick ✓ the things in the list you think they had to do.

1 Swim underwater ☐
2 Watch different channels on TV ☐
3 Go to the doctor for a health check ☐
4 Do a lot of exercise ☐
5 Sleep less than usual ☐
6 Learn about space ☐
7 Stay in bed all day ☐
8 Eat only chocolate cake ☐

3 What special things do you think Elena and Luca took with them into space? Write three ideas and then share them with a partner.

I think they took a camera so they could take lots of photos of Earth!

4 What would you take into space? Share your ideas with a partner.

5 **Look at the three pictures. Write about this story. Write 20 or more words.**

1 Read the story. Choose a word from the box. Write the correct word next to numbers 1–5. There is one example.

example				
space	deep	people	shelf	repairing
screen	ran	banks	flew	astronauts

Last Friday Betty was preparing to go into ___space___ in an enormous rocket. First, she met the other astronauts in her team, Oliver and Helen. Betty checked their helmets. 'We mustn't make a mistake because our trip is for two months,' she told the team. Oliver suddenly remembered his gloves, so he (**1**) ____________ quickly back to his office to fetch them. The rocket was nearly ready to leave!

At nine o'clock, they sat in their places. Betty wasn't worried because this was her tenth journey. She touched a (**2**) ____________ and turned on different machines. The engine started and soon the team were on their way to an unusual planet called I-654-073K. 'I feel sick,' said Helen. It was only her second trip. She felt better after they (**3**) ____________ past the moon.

The team arrived, they explored the planet and collected some colourful rocks. The rocks helped Betty to explain why there weren't any (**4**) ____________ on I-654-073K.

There is going to be a party with scientists when the (**5**) ____________ come back and Betty and her team are going to be on the news on TV!

2 Now choose the best name for the story. Tick one box.

Helen feels ill ☐
Rocks from the moon ☐
Well done, Betty's team! ☐

1 Read the instructions. Play the game.

INSTRUCTIONS

Choose four pictures. Write the words in your notebook. You must collect these.

Roll the dice and move.

Collect your four words. Tick ✓ them in your notebook.

On green squares, say the word.

On ? squares, answer the question on the card.

On orange squares, say the past participle of the verb and spell it.

9 Great bakers

DIVERSICUS

My unit goals

- I want to ______________________________
____
- To do this, I will ______________________________
____
- I will say and write ____ new words.

My mission diary

How was it? Draw a face.

1

2

3

My favourite stage:

____

I can talk about mealtimes, snacks and cooking. ☐

I can say what things look, feel, sound, smell or taste like. ☐

I can say what makes me angry, sad or happy. ☐

I can read and complete a text with the correct grammatical words. ☐

I completed Level 4 Unit 9. ☐

Go to page 12(and add to you word stack!

1 Look and complete the crossword.

2 Match. Write the mealtime words and past participles

1 bo bowl rk
bo bought oon

2 sp ______ ~~wl~~
sp ______ own

3 kn ______ oken
kn ______ rgotten

4 fo ______ ~~ught~~
fo ______ ife

Sounds and spelling

3 4.43 Listen and circle the words with the *sh* sound in them.

snack delicious ocean station shampoo
chess sugar sure cheap shelf

4 Complete the words with the letters.

sh ci ti

1 space __ __ ip
2 fire sta __ __ on
3 musi __ __ an

1 Choose words from the box to complete the sentences. You do not need to use all the words.

~~music~~ delicious May expensive olives like rice unusual Grandpa lots outside

1 Grandpa thinks the __music__ sounds nice.
2 They put on caps and sun cream because they're going to eat ________.
3 The sun cream smells ________ coconut.
4 Grandpa and Grandma are sitting on an ________ rug.
5 Jim tells Grandma how people eat ________ in South Korea.
6 ________ doesn't like olives.

2 Circle the correct words.

Su-Lin's Diary

What a great day we've [1]**had / have**! We're back home now and we had a party to say 'goodbye' for the [2]**end / entrance** of the tour.

We've [3]**brought / sold** lots of things back from our trip, and we used [4]**any / some** of them for the party. We thought the music from Dubai [5]**tasted / sounded** wonderful. Mr Friendly showed Jim and Jenny's [6]**parents / grandparents** the unusual rug which he found in Egypt. He was very pleased with it because it [7]**was / wasn't** cheap.

Jim and Jenny's grandpa tried to eat noodles with the chopsticks which we got in South Korea, but he decided it was difficult ... but the [8]**funnier / funniest** moment was when he thought the olives were grapes because they looked like grapes. He didn't like them at all and he said they were horrible!.

Well, diary, this is the last day from this tour. Goodbye for now.

3 Review the story.

I think the story is **great / good / OK / not very good**.
My favourite character is ________.
My favourite part is when ________________.

1 Read and answer.

Katy was happy. That afternoon a girl in her class was having a party and she felt excited because she had an invitation. She was getting ready. While she was getting ready, she picked up her soap from the shelf in the bathroom. It looked like a rabbit, but it smelt like flowers. She loved it. While she was having a shower, she also used her mum's expensive shampoo to wash her hair. The shampoo was called 'Butterfly Wings' and it smelt like fruit and chocolate.

After her shower, Katy put on her costume. She dressed up like a piece of pizza.

Her mum smiled when she saw her and she said, 'You look delicious, and you smell good enough to eat! It smells like you've used my shampoo!'

'Yes, I have,' said Katy. 'It makes me feel good. I feel like a queen.'

'Yes, you look like the Queen of Pizzas,' her mum laughed.

1 Who was having a party? A girl in Katy's class.
2 What did Katy pick up while she was getting ready? ______
3 What did her soap look like? ______
4 What did she use to wash her hair? ______
5 What did the shampoo smell like? ______
6 What did Katy put on after her shower? ______
7 What did she feel like? ______

2 Put the words in order. Write the sentences.

1 like oranges and | These biscuits taste | delicious! | coconuts. They're

These biscuits taste like oranges and coconuts. They're delicious!

2 was raining. | unhappy because it | looked | The children

______

3 like | This cheese | yesterday's socks! | smells

______

4 feels like | cat. | This blanket | a furry

______

5 whispering. | like people | wind sounds | That soft

______

1 Write the words in the correct column.

~~cook~~ ~~milk~~ ~~spoon~~ ~~sugar~~ mix eggs knife wash up yoghurt boil rice jam butter fork bake scissors ice cream flour oven cheese

Verbs	Dairy	Ingredients	Things we use
cook	milk	sugar	spoon

2 Put the sentences in order.

Ingredients
250 g soft butter 140 g sugar 1 egg yolk (the yellow part) 300 g flour lemon zest

a [ ] Wash up, make sure you leave a clean and tidy kitchen and enjoy the biscuits.
b [ ] After 30 minutes, take out the mixture and cut it into the shapes which you want. The biscuits can be circles, squares or rectangles.
c [1] First, mix the butter and sugar in a large bowl. Use a wooden spoon.
d [ ] Put the biscuits on a metal tray and put them carefully into the oven. Bake for 12–15 minutes.
e [ ] Secondly, add the egg yolk and lemon zest and mix together quickly.
f [ ] When the mixture is in the fridge, turn on the oven and heat it to 180°C.
g [ ] Then slowly add the flour and mix it all together. Use your hands to help you.
h [ ] Use oven gloves to take them out of the oven and let them cool for 10 minutes.
i [ ] Put all the mixture in a plastic bag and leave it in the fridge until it is cold.

1 Complete the sentences with the words in the box.

~~unhappy~~	tired	thirsty	hungry	bored	angry	happy	frightened

1 Watching bad news on TV made my dad unhappy .
2 People who are unkind to animals make me ______ .
3 Our uncle was baking bread in the kitchen. The smell made us ______ .
4 Listening to her favourite pop music makes her ______ .
5 The hot dry desert made the explorer ______ .
6 Travelling by car on a motorway for a long time makes us ______ .
7 Going on fast rides at the funfair makes him ______ .
8 Playing football all afternoon has made them ______ .

2 Find six differences. Write sentences.

In picture A he's tidied the kitchen, but in picture B he hasn't tidied it yet.

______

______

______

______

______

1 Read about tea. Look at the tea bags 1–5. Where do sentences a–e go in the text? Write the numbers.

Tea grows on large pieces of land called plantations. The best place to grow tea is on high land in the mountains because tea bushes need a lot of rain and they don't like a lot of sun. 1

When the tea bushes are three years old, the plantation workers choose the smallest, youngest leaves from each plant. 2 Some plantations use machines to pick the leaves, but many plantations prefer people to pick the leaves.

They send the tea to a factory. The leaves have a lot of water in them. Workers put the tea on large shelves and leave them to dry in warm air. Now the leaves are about 60–70% water. 3 They put the broken leaves in a room for between half an hour and two hours. 4 The green leaves change to light brown and then darker brown. This makes kinds of tea that all taste different.

They use hot air to dry the leaves until they are only about 3% water. 5 These tea chests go to different factories where they make tea bags or they put the loose tea into boxes to sell in shops.

a ☐ In this room, oxygen changes the colour of the leaves.
b 1 The plants grow more slowly there, but the tea tastes better.
c ☐ They pick the leaves carefully so that they do not hurt the plant.
d ☐ Workers pack the tea into special boxes called tea chests.
e ☐ Next, machines called rollers break the leaves.

2 Compare the production of tea to the production of chocolate.

1 Tea plants are bushes, but ______________________________.
2 We use the leaves of the tea plant, but ______________________________.
3 Tea plants need cool temperatures, but ______________________________
______________________________.

3 **People in the UK like food from many different countries. Use the internet to find out where these meals come from.**

1 Paella comes from _____Spain_____.

2 Chicken korma comes from __________.

3 Pad Thai comes from __________.

4 Guacamole comes from __________.

5 Dim sum comes from __________.

6 Sushi comes from __________.

4 **Complete the descriptions of these traditional foods from the UK. Match them with the photos.**

1 __________ is a delicious English dessert. It's very easy to make. It's made of cakes, jelly, fruit, custard and cream.

2 This is a __________ cake. It's made with butter, eggs, sugar and flour. In the middle, there's jam and sometimes cream.

3 __________ has meat and vegetables at the bottom. Above that, there are mashed potatoes.

a

b

c

1 Order the events from the gingerbread girl story.

a

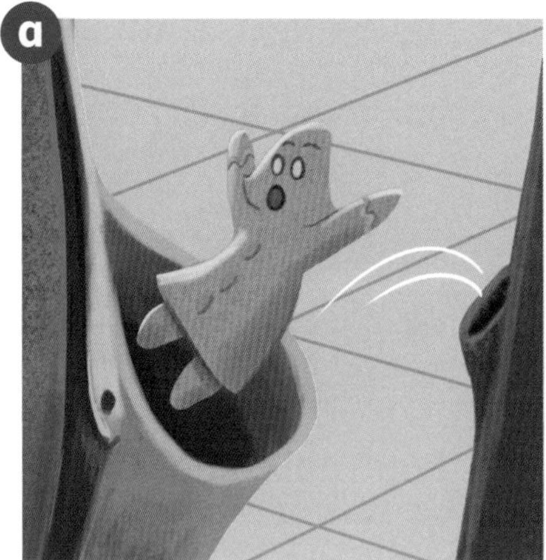

[ ] The gingerbread girl jumps into Mrs Brett's handbag and escapes.

b

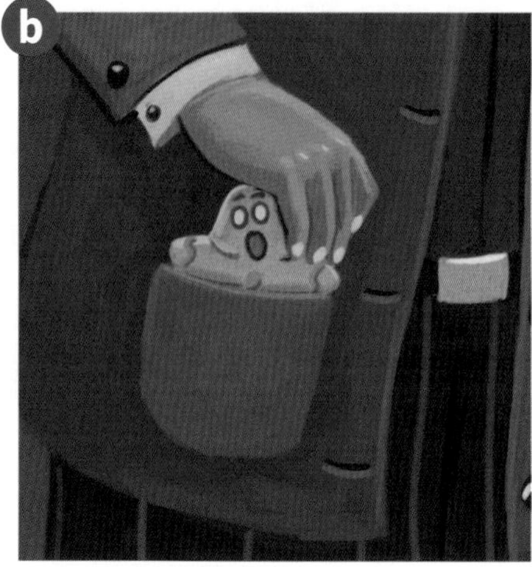

[ ] Mr Brett puts a gingerbread girl in his pocket.

c

[ ] Bruno gives the gingerbread to the people at Spring Wood.

d

[ ] The gingerbread girl sees Bruno from the bus and runs to him.

e

[1] Bruno makes gingerbread people.

f

[ ] Mr Brett comes to Bruno's house.

2 Write about something you made or did with love for someone. Who was it for? What was it? Draw a picture.

____

____

____

____

3 4.44 **Listen and draw lines. There is one example.**

Lucy Charlie Sarah

Robert Katy Helen Nick

1 **Read the letter and write the missing words.**
Write one word on each line.

Example	We're having an amazing time in the mountains.
1	We've made some jam and tomorrow we're going ______ visit
	a village to see some bees. We're going to learn how they make honey!
2	Yesterday, we met a friend of Mum's while we ______ walking in
3	the mountains. He's a cook here. He invited ______ to his
	restaurant to make some biscuits. They smelt delicious when they were
4	cooking in the oven. They tasted better ______
	the ones we usually buy in the supermarket. Later, we tidied the kitchen
	and walked to our hotel in the square. The walk made us hungry,
5	______ Mum and I ate an enormous pizza.

1 Read the instructions. Play the game.

FINISH

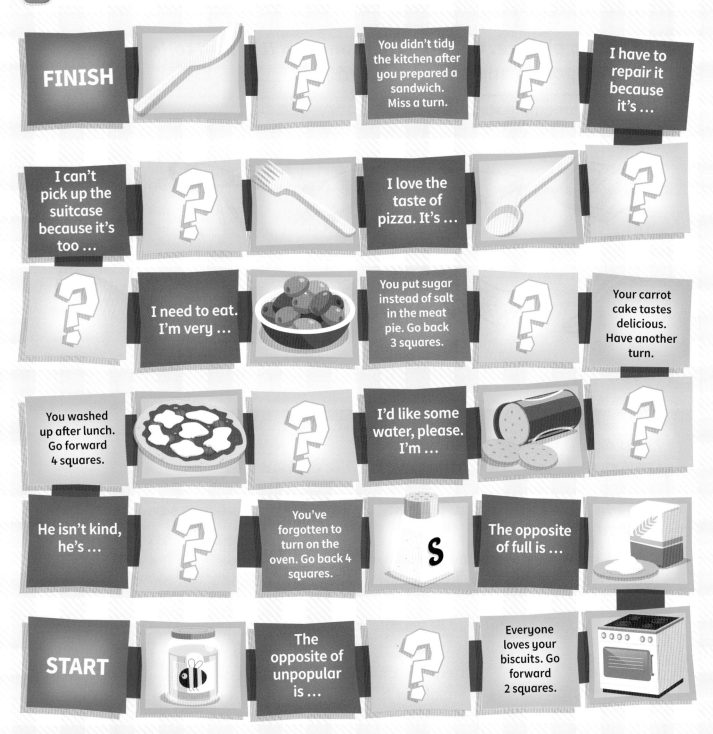

You didn't tidy the kitchen after you prepared a sandwich. Miss a turn.

I have to repair it because it's …

I can't pick up the suitcase because it's too …

I love the taste of pizza. It's …

I need to eat. I'm very …

You put sugar instead of salt in the meat pie. Go back 3 squares.

Your carrot cake tastes delicious. Have another turn.

You washed up after lunch. Go forward 4 squares.

I'd like some water, please. I'm …

He isn't kind, he's …

You've forgotten to turn on the oven. Go back 4 squares.

S

The opposite of full is …

START

The opposite of unpopular is …

Everyone loves your biscuits. Go forward 2 squares.

INSTRUCTIONS

Roll the dice and move.

On green squares, say the word.

On ? squares, answer the question on the card.

On purple squares, complete the sentence with an adjective.

Review ● ● ● Units 7–9

1 **Choose a picture. Give a definition with *It's used to/for*. Your partner points and says the word.**

It's used for eating soup.

A spoon!

2 **Read Sophia's story. Find and write the words for feelings.**

Last night, I had a dream that I was an astronaut. I was in a rocket and I was going to another planet. I remember it made me feel frightened, but also excited.

'You're going to arrive on the planet and you're going to stay there for two years,' another astronaut told me. I felt sad when I was saying goodbye to my family and friends.

When I arrived, I started to explore and I was surprised to find an enormous hole with something in it. 'That looks like a spaceship,' I thought as I looked down. I went back to my rocket to fetch my torch. I stood in front of the spaceship and touched the door.

Suddenly, someone (or something!?) opened the door and it (or they) turned on a light. An unusual voice said, 'Will you stay here and save us?'

'It smells like biscuits,' I thought. 'Is someone baking in there?' This made me feel happy, not afraid.

I don't remember the rest of the dream, but I felt very hungry when I woke up! Dreams are strange, aren't they?

frightened, ______________________________

3 Read Sophia's story again. Correct the sentences.

1 Sophia is an astronaut.
Sophia was an astronaut in her dream.

2 The dream made her feel unhappy.

3 She felt sad when she was exploring the planet.

4 She found an empty hole.

5 She found the entrance and she opened the door.

6 She felt worried when she smelt the biscuits.

7 She thinks dreams are boring.

4 Plan a story starting with *Last night I had a dream that I was an astronaut.*

- Where were you going?
- How long are you going to stay there?
- How did you feel?
- What did you see/smell/hear?

5 Write your story. Use your notes from Activity 4.

CHECK!
Have you answered all the questions in Activity 4?
Have you used the format of a story?
Have you used the correct vocabulary and grammar?
Is your spelling correct?

1 Write your favourite new words.

Kathryn Escribano

With Caroline Nixon and Michael Tomlinson

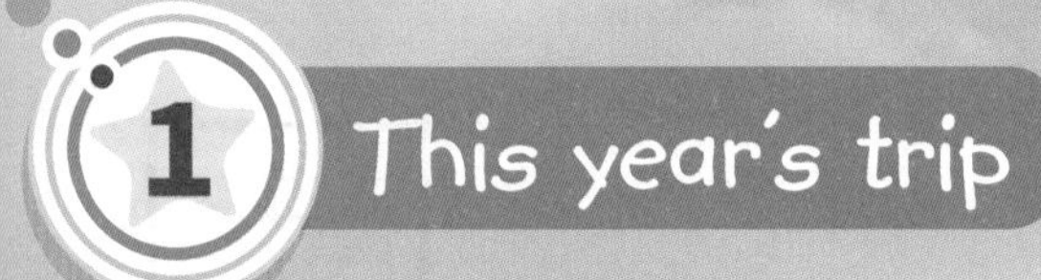

1 This year's trip

Birthday maths!

When's Katy's birthday? Do the maths and find out!

Katy's birthday is in the **eighth** / **ninth** / **tenth** month.
The name of this month is _______________.

Funny English

In your dreams

You can say 'in your dreams' when you think something is impossible.

I think all the shops are open on 1st January.

Ha! In your dreams.

Is there a similar phrase in your language?

Did you know?

The word 'calendar' comes from the Latin word *Kalendae*. It means 'the first day of the month.'

Which word does your birthday month come from?

Guess what it is

taxi ambulance motorway platform railway station ~~bicycle~~

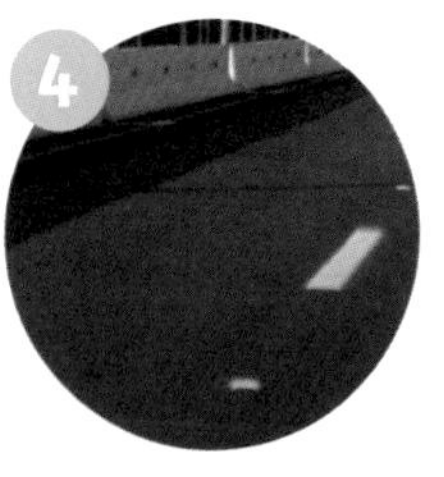

1 It may be a bicycle.
2 ______
3 ______
4 ______
5 ______
6 ______

Window to the World

Burj Al Arab is a luxury hotel on an artificial island in Dubai. It looks like a huge ship sail → . There's a restaurant under the sea and a helipad (a space for a helicopter) → .

In 2005, two famous tennis players played on the hotel helipad. Who were they? Find out!

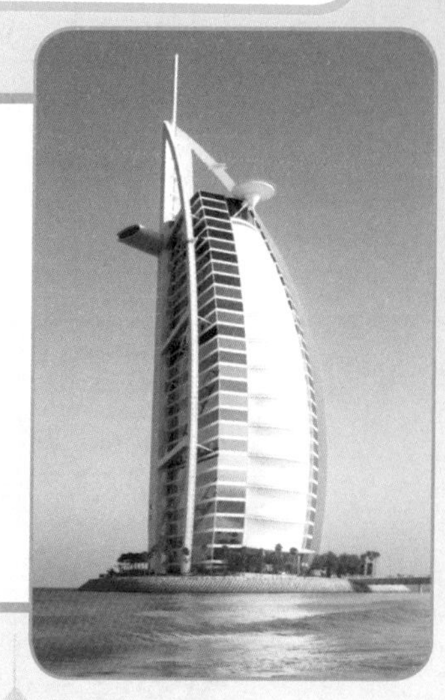

Home mission

Design a luxury hotel.

- Ask three people at home for ideas. What has the hotel got? What does it look like? Where is it? You can use the words in the box.

swimming pools restaurants shops cinemas gyms

- Draw your hotel, give it a name and describe it.

This is the 'Silver Hotel'. It's got two swimming pools and four restaurants. There are …

2 Our beautiful planet

Natural world wordsearch

Find 11 more words. Circle the animal words blue and the natural places green.

j	s	t	r	e	a	m	l	w	p	o
t	o	r	t	o	i	s	e	o	h	c
o	l	c	c	h	i	w	c	o	i	t
c	l	a	n	d	e	a	a	d	a	o
e	x	v	o	r	o	n	m	u	n	p
a	d	e	s	e	r	t	e	n	c	u
n	f	t	n	e	a	g	l	e	s	s
l	a	v	i	b	e	e	t	l	e	e

Funny English

It's raining cats and dogs!

You can say 'It's raining cats and dogs!' when it's raining a lot.

Let's stay at home.
It's raining cats and dogs!

What do you do when it's raining cats and dogs?

Window to the World

Some words that Australians use are different from the words that people use in the UK.

What do these Australian English words mean?

1 G'day! — b Hello!
2 Ta.
3 mate
4 barbie

a Thanks.
b Hello!
c barbecue
d friend

an Australian 'barbie'

Are there different words for the same thing in your language?

Picture instructions

- Read the instructions and find, circle and write three more mistakes in Michael's picture.
- Read the instructions again and draw the picture in your notebook.

Instructions

On the right, draw three trees. In the sky above the trees, draw four butterflies. On the left, draw a stream, and a swan swimming in it. Next to the stream, on the grass, draw six stones. At the back, draw three hills and draw a cave in the second hill.

1 *There aren't enough trees.*

2 There are too many ______.

3 ______

4 ______

Home mission

With people at home, match the places and animals from Australia to the descriptions. Which is your favourite place? Which is your favourite animal? Ask the people at home what they prefer.

a Uluru b Kangaroo Island c koalas d emus

1 These marsupials sleep for more than 20 hours a day! ☐

2 These are the largest birds in Australia. ☐

3 Another name for this huge red rock formation is Ayers Rock. ☐

4 Koalas, penguins and kangaroos live there. ☐

Which is your favourite place?

It's Kangaroo Island.

3 Let's celebrate!

Have you ever ... ?

- Circle *Yes* or *No*. Then count your points and read your result.
- **Yes** = 2 points **No** = 1 point

- **Have you ever visited another country? Yes / No**
- **Have you ever travelled by plane? Yes / No**
- **Have you ever eaten food from another country? Yes / No**
- **Have you ever spoken to someone from another country? Yes / No**
- **Do you like learning about other countries? Yes / No**
- **Have you ever watched a film from another country? Yes / No**

Points

- **10–12 points:** You've had lots of experiences about different countries. You've been lucky!
- **7–9 points:** You've had some experiences about different countries. Why don't you look for more?
- **6 points:** You haven't had many experiences about different countries yet, but there may be some in the future. Enjoy them when they come!

Window to the World

Capoeira is a Brazilian activity with dance, music and martial arts. People often play capoeira in a circle called a 'roda'.

Are there any sports or activities that come from your country?

What do the crazy words mean?

volleyball

chess

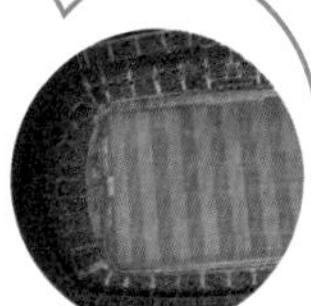
stadium

violin

drum

instruments

- stadrum: *stadium + drum = a stadium where you play the drums*
- volleyments: ______________________
- instruchess: ______________________
- vioball: ______________________
- volleydium: ______________________
- drumlin: ______________________

Funny English

It rings a bell.

If something 'rings a bell', you can remember it, but not fully.

*Your name **rings a bell**. Did we play volleyball last year?*

Is there a similar phrase in your language?

Did you know?

Chess comes from India. People first played chess 1500 years ago!

What's the English name for your favourite chess piece?

Home mission

Who sings best at home? Ask three people to sing *Happy Birthday* (or another song that you like). Then sing the song yourself. Give everyone a score out of 10 and see who's the winner!

4 Time of our lives

Emma, David or Holly?

My name's **Emma**. I was born in London, but now I live in Bath. I'm ten and I've played tennis since I was seven. I love sports! I haven't got a pet. Last July, I went to Colombia with my family. I met my cousins there. It was great!

I'm **David** and I'm ten. I was born in Bath in the house where I live now. I've got a dog, Tess. I've had Tess since I was four and I love looking after her. I play the drums. I began when I was six. I love music!

My name's **Holly** and I'm nine years old. I've lived in Bath all my life but in two different houses. Two years ago, I began to play the violin and a year ago I started tennis lessons. I like music and sport, but I don't like preparing for exams!

1 ___David___ has always lived in the same house.

2 ____________ has played tennis for three years.

3 ____________ has had a pet for six years.

4 ____________ is learning to play an instrument and a sport.

5 ____________ has been to a different country.

6 ____________ has played tennis for a year.

Funny English

race against the clock

You 'race against the clock' when you do something quickly because there isn't enough time.

This homework is for tomorrow.
*I'm **racing against the clock** to finish it!*

When was the last time you raced against the clock?

Did you know?

Bogotá is one of the highest capital cities in the world.

Which is the highest city in your country?

What was the time?

Read Katy's note and look at the pictures. Can you draw the hands on Katy's clocks?

Yesterday was a busy day! While I was sleeping, Michael was having breakfast. While I was tidying my room, Michael was preparing for his maths exam. And while Michael was repairing his bike, I was looking after my brother.

Window to the World

Colombia is famous for its coffee. Have you ever seen a coffee plant?

Look at the picture of the coffee beans. Which fruit do they look like? Circle.

Coffee beans look like **strawberries / mangoes / grapes.**

What food or drink is your country famous for?

coffee beans on a coffee plant

Home mission

Look at the times from Michael's clocks and write three more times. Write what you were doing yesterday at these times. Then ask someone at home and write their answers. Were you doing the same thing at any of the times?

8:10 in the morning 4:25 in the afternoon 5:45 in the afternoon

What were you doing yesterday at ten past eight in the morning?

I was having a shower.

Let it snow!

Storyboard

- Choose a number between two and six.
- Start on 'spring' and move around the board. Cross out the words you stop on. For example, if you choose number 3, cross out 'autumn' and then 'foggy'.
- Keep going around the storyboard, moving the number of squares you have chosen. Jump over the crossed out words and cross out new ones. When you have one word of each colour, make a crazy sentence!
- Repeat the game. Choose a different number each time.

It's spring and there's ice. Michael says 'I'll swim in the pond'.

START →

spring	summer	autumn	winter

warm
foggy
storm
ice

Katy	Jim	Michael	Betty

I'll make a snowman.
I'll go to the beach.
I'll swim in the pond.
I'll go skiing.

Did you know?

Argentina's name comes from the Latin word *argentum*, which means 'silver'. It's the only country in the world named after a metal.

What's the origin of the name of your country?

Window to the World

The Perito Moreno Glacier (*Glaciar Perito Moreno*) is in the southwest of Argentina. It's one of the most beautiful places to visit in Patagonia. A glacier is a huge body of ice.

Do glaciers move? Find out!

Match the joke parts

Why did the melon jump into the pond?

Why was the maths book sad?

Why do birds fly south in winter?

Why did Katy throw the clock out of the window?

Why didn't the skeleton go to the dance?

Because it's easier than walking!

Because it had many problems!

Because he had noBODY to go with!

So it could become a WATERmelon!

So she could see time fly!

Choose your favourite joke and draw it in your notebook. Show it at home!

Funny English

get cold feet

You 'get cold feet' when you become too frightened to do something you wanted to do.

*I wanted to learn snowboarding, but I **got cold feet**!*

Have you ever got cold feet?

Home mission

Do you change your clocks in spring and autumn? What happens to the light in the mornings and evenings when the clocks change? Is changing the clocks a good idea? Ask three people at home.

Do you think changing the clocks in spring is a good idea?

Yes, I think it is.

Break the jobs code

Use the code to write the jobs. Then write the code for three more jobs.

	A	B	C	D	E
1	a	b	c	d	e
2	f	g	h	i	j
3	k	l	m	n	o
4	p	q	r	s	t
5	u	v	w	x	y

1 1E – 3D – 2B – 2D – 3D – 1E – 1E – 4C = engineer

2 4A – 2D – 3B – 3E – 4E = ____________

3 3C – 1E – 1C – 2C – 1A – 3D – 2D – 1C = ____________

4 ____________

5 ____________

6 ____________

Window to the World

Taekwondo is a South Korean martial art with high kicks and jumps. Its name comes from the Korean words *tae* = foot; *kwon* = fist → and *do* = way of. Taekwondo means 'the way of the foot and fist'.

Another martial art from South Korea starts with the letter *H*. What's its name? What does the name mean?

snowed under

You are 'snowed under' when you have too much work.

*My aunt needs help. She's **snowed under** with work!*

What can you do if you feel snowed under?

What are they saying?

Write the sentences. Then match the short questions to the sentences.

already / my / I've / prepared / school uniform

~~I / my / before / tidied / room / I / to bed / went~~

not / I'm / the / watching / football match

cake / the / I / eat / didn't

a Didn't you?
b Have you?
~~c Did you?~~
d Aren't you?

1

I tidied my room before I went to bed.

c

2

3

4

Ask four people at home what they wanted to be when they were children. Compare their answers with the jobs they have now. Is anyone doing the job they wanted to do when they were young? What would you like to be when you grow up?

What did you want to be when you were a child?

I wanted to be a pilot.
I loved planes!

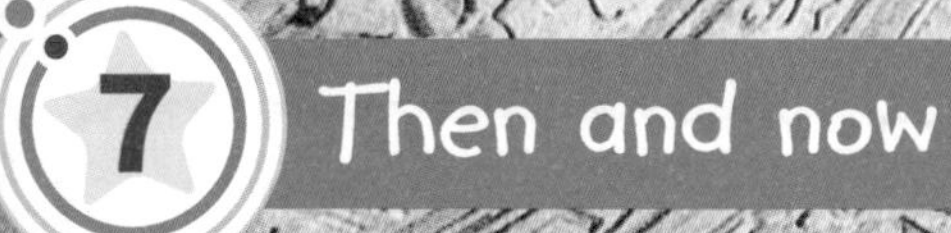

Things in the home sudoku

Write the missing words. The same word can't be on the same line → ↓ or in the same rectangle.

comb		brush			key
	fridge			________	
oven			soap		________
________		________	________		
________	________		________	________	________
			________	________	

Did you know?

People started using combs about 5,000 years ago. The ancient Egyptians made combs out of wood.

Have you got a comb? What colour is it?

Funny English

brush up

If you 'brush up on' something, you study and practise it.

*I'm going to **brush up on my English** before my trip to London.*

Do you have to brush up on something this week?

ENGLISH

Crazy definitions!

- Play and write definitions. You need a dice, a pencil and paper.
- Tick (✓) or put a cross (✗).

What's a fridge used for? It's used for brushing your hair. ✗

What's a fridge used for?

What's a brush used for?

What's an oven used for?

What's a key used for?

What's shampoo used for?

What's a telephone used for?

It's used for brushing your hair.

It's used for cooking food.

It's used to keep food fresh.

It's used to wash your hair.

It's used to open a door.

It's used to speak to someone in another place.

Window to the World

About 5,000 years ago, the ancient Egyptians started to use hieroglyphs to write. A hieroglyph is a picture that represents a sound or a word. The people who wrote were called 'scribes', and they started learning to write hieroglyphs when they were 6.

Can you write your name using the hieroglyphs in the chart?

Home mission

Use the hieroglyphs chart on this page to write the names of four people at home. Then show them the names. Can they guess whose name is whose?

I think this one is my name.

Yes, it is!

8 Space travel

Amazing rocket

Circle eight more space words in the rocket. When you find an extra letter, write it below. What's the mystery word?

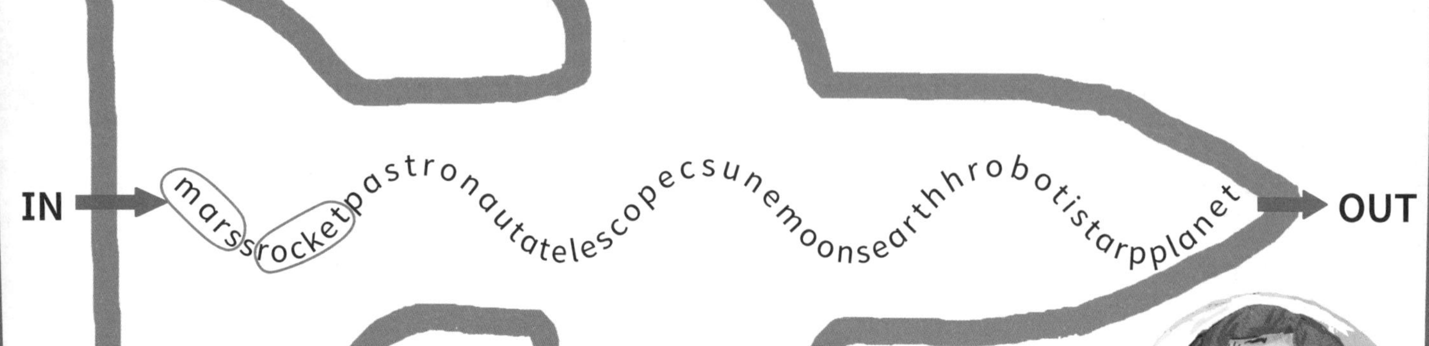

The mystery word is s________________.

Window to the World

The ancient Romans named most of the planets in our solar system. Only one planet got its name from the ancient Greeks. **Which one is it?**

Find out and circle it.

Mercury Venus Earth Mars Jupiter Saturn Uranus Neptune

Funny English

once in a blue moon

You do something 'once in a blue moon' when you don't do it very often.

My grandma turns on the TV ***once in a blue moon.*** *She doesn't like it.*

What do you do once in a blue moon?

Space calculator

- You need a calculator, a pencil and paper.
- Read the instructions and do the maths. What are you in space to discover?

1 Your spaceship has the number 1569. Put this number on your calculator.
2 You are going to go into space on 28th May, so add 2805 → **1569 + 2805**
3 Your spaceship has got three parts, so multiply by 3 → **1569 + 2805 x 3**
4 It's time for leaving and counting down! So subtract 10 → **1569 + 2805 x 3 – 10**
5 You're travelling with two astronauts, so multiply by 2 → **1569 + 2805 x 3 – 10 x 2**
6 There are 8 planets in our solar system, so add 8 → **1569 + 2805 x 3 – 10 x 2 + 8**
7 The International Space Station is 350 kilometres above the earth, so add 350 → **1569 + 2805 x 3 – 10 x 2 + 8 + 350**
8 350 kilometres is 218 miles, so add 218 → **1569 + 2805 x 3 – 10 x 2 + 8 + 350 + 218**
9 After 2 days, you get to the ISS, so multiply by 2 → **1569 + 2805 x 3 – 10 x 2 + 8 + 350 + 218 x 2**
10 You go around the Earth 16 times a day: that's 64 times in 4 days. Add 64 → **1569 + 2805 x 3 – 10 x 2 + 8 + 350 + 218 x 2 + 64**
11 You fall asleep and dream that you're 40! So add 40 → **1569 + 2805 x 3 – 10 x 2 + 8 + 350 + 218 x 2 + 64 + 40**

- Write the result of your sum here: ______________
- Now, use this chart to break the code and write the word. The word is ______________ .

0	3	4	5	7
e	o	s	h	l

- Use the word above to complete what you are in space to discover.
  I'm in space to discover black ______________ .

Home mission

Play the planets game.

- With people at home, practise this sentence to remember the order of the planets in English. The first letter of each word is the first letter of each planet.

My Very Enthusiastic Mother Just Served Us Noodles!

- Close your Home Booklet. Can you all say the names of the planets in order?

9 Great bakers

What's wrong?

Look at the ingredients to make English scones. Look at the picture. What's wrong?

English scones

225 grams of flour
¼ teaspoon of salt
3 teaspoons of baking powder
50 grams of butter
25 grams of sugar
150 millilitres of milk
1 egg

1 *There isn't enough flour.*
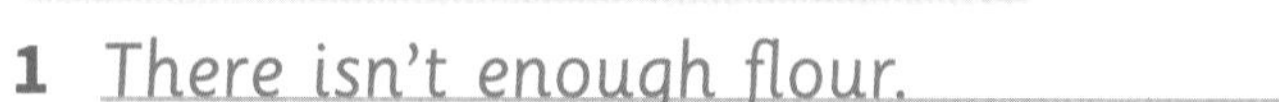

2 There's too much ________________.

3 ________________

4 ________________

5 ________________

6 ________________

Window to the World

'Slang' is informal words and phrases that people use. Cockney rhyming slang comes from the east of London and uses words that rhyme. For example, *biscuits and cheese* means *knees* (*cheese* rhymes with *knees*).

What do these phrases mean? Circle the correct word. It has to rhyme!

Jam tart means **spoon / heart**.
Plates of meat means **feet / legs**.

biscuits and cheese = knees

Funny English

a piece of cake

Something is 'a piece of cake' when it's very easy.

I did my homework in ten minutes because it was a piece of cake!

What's a piece of cake for you?

Emotions pizza!

Complete each piece of pizza with your ideas. You can use these words:

makes me ... hungry happy sad excited angry frightened thirsty

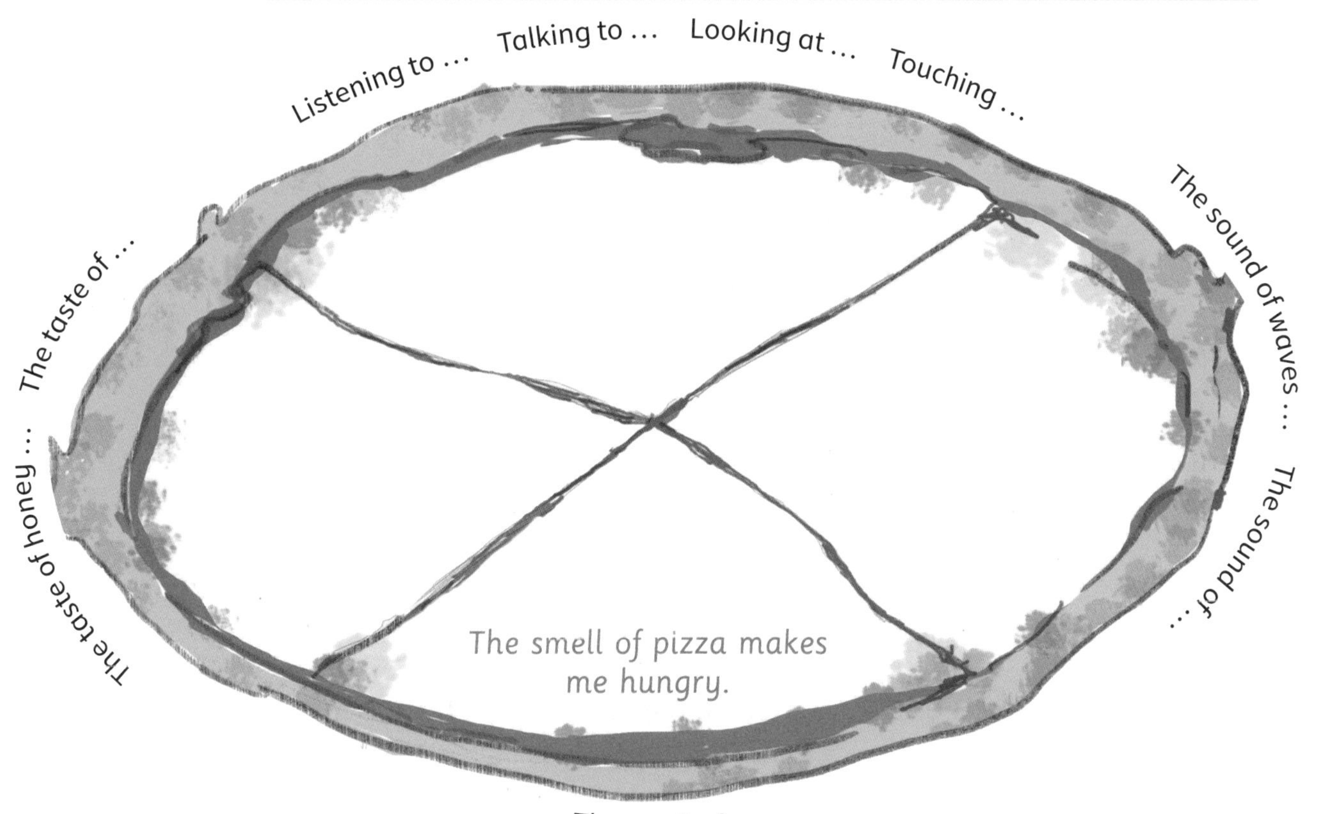

Listening to ...
Talking to ...
Looking at ...
Touching ...
The sound of waves ...
The sound of ...
The smell of pizza makes me hungry.
The smell of ...
The taste of honey ...
The taste of ...

Home mission

What's your favourite sandwich got in it? Write your answer. Then ask three people at home and compare their answers with your own. Are any of the ingredients the same?

What has your favourite sandwich got in it?

It's got cheese, olives and ...

Which of the sandwiches makes you hungry? Make it and enjoy it!

Did you know?

The inventor of the sandwich was British. His name was the Earl of Sandwich. He wanted to have a quick lunch, so he asked for 'a piece of meat between two pieces of bread'.

Find out about a snack from your country. Who invented it?

Ordinal numbers

1st	2nd	3rd	4th	5th	6th
first	second	third	fourth	fifth	sixth

7th	8th	9th	10th	11th
seventh	eighth	ninth	tenth	eleventh
12th	13th	14th	15th	16th
twelfth	thirteenth	fourteenth	fifteenth	sixteenth
17th	18th	19th	20th	21st
seventeenth	eighteenth	nineteenth	twentieth	twenty-first
22nd	23rd	24th	25th	26th
twenty-second	twenty-third	twenty-fourth	twenty-fifth	twenty-sixth
27th	28th	29th	30th	31st
twenty-seventh	twenty-eighth	twenty-ninth	thirtieth	thirty-first

When's your birthday?
Think of three people at home. When are their birthdays?

Months

Jan Feb Mar Apr May Jun

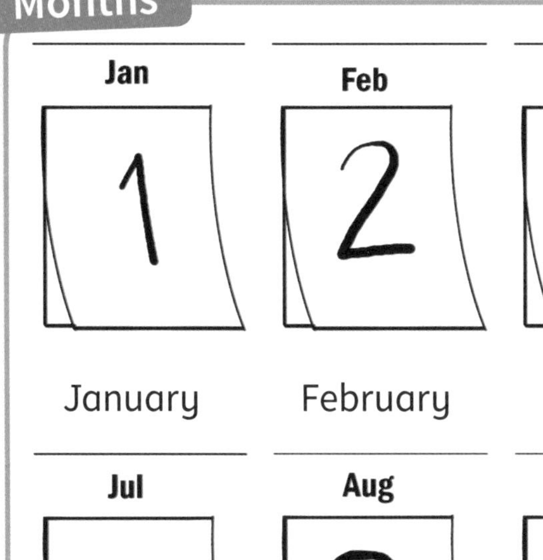

1 2 3 4 5 6

January February March April May June

Jul Aug Sep Oct Nov Dec

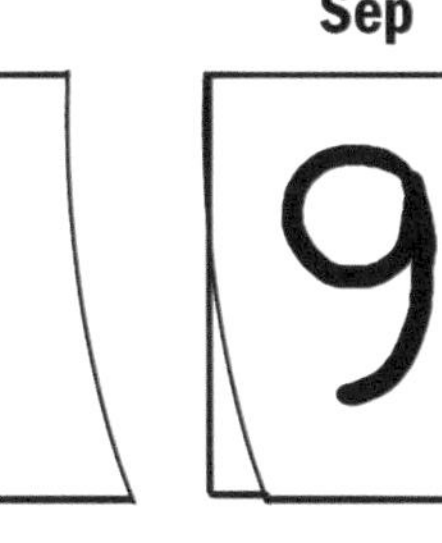

7 8 9 10 11 12

July August September October November December

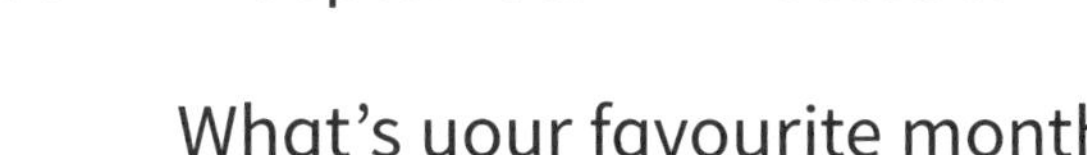

What's your favourite month?

Journeys

ambulance

bicycle

motorway

passenger

platform

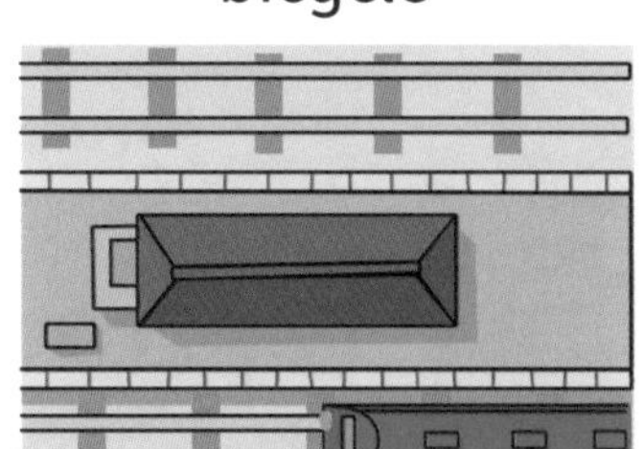

railway

taxi

traffic

Can you think of five more journey and transport words?

The natural world

cave desert environment fire hill(s)

land ocean stone stream wood(s)

 Imagine your ideal natural place. What can you see there? 

Animals

beetle butterfly camel creature dinosaur

eagle extinct octopus swan tortoise

Where can you see these animals? Which of these animals is extinct?

Competitions

chess

match

prize

puzzle

quiz

race

score

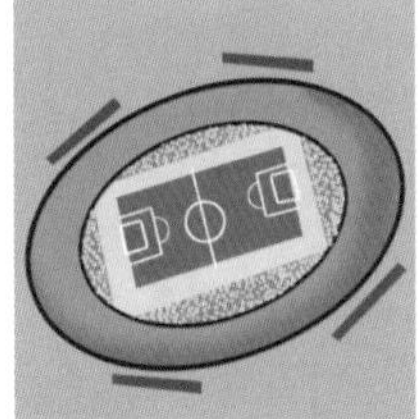
stadium

team

volleyball

winner

Have you ever played in a team?

Music and festivals

concert

drum

festival

flag

instrument(s)

musician

pop

rock

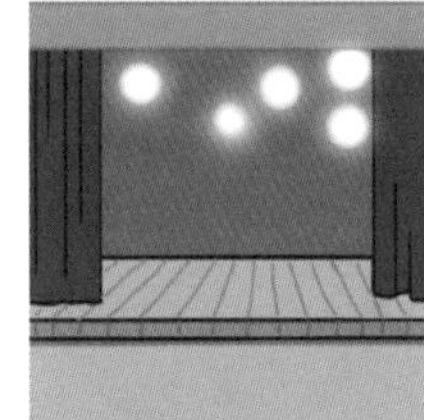
stage

tune

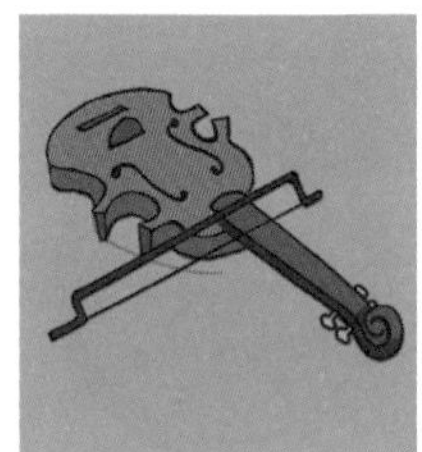
violin

whistle

What's your favourite type of music? What can you see at festivals in your country?

Verbs for offers, promises and requests

fetch

look after

make sure

meet

prepare

repair

send

tidy

 Which things did you do last week? Choose five. 

Telling the time

five past three

ten past three

quarter past three

twenty past three

twenty-five past three

twenty-five to four

twenty to four

quarter to four

ten to four

five to four

a.m.

p.m.

 What were you doing at … ? Choose five times. 

Seasons and weather

spring

summer

autumn

winter

fog/foggy

ice

storm

warm

What's your favourite season? Do you see storms in your country?

In winter

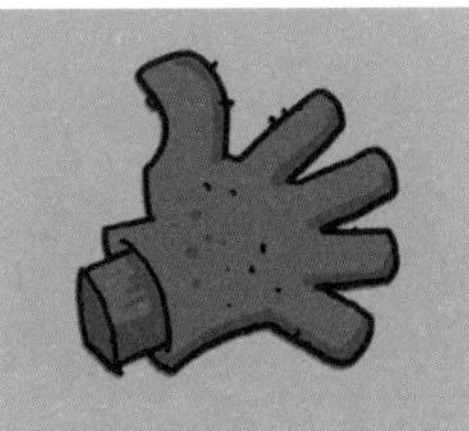
glove

pocket

pond

skiing

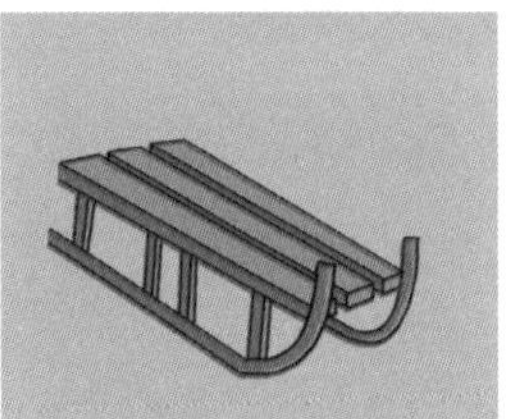
sledge

snowball

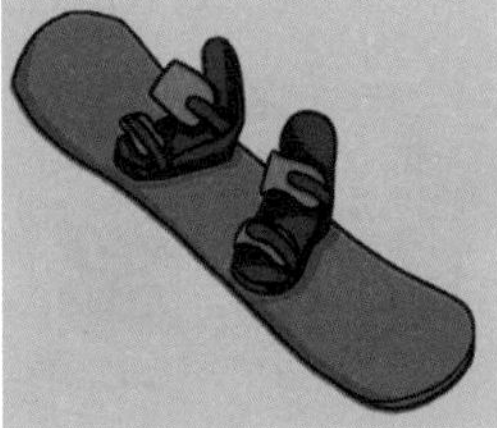
snowboard

snowboarding

snowman

What will you do this winter? Say five things.

Jobs

businessman/
businesswoman

engineer

firefighter

manager

mechanic

pilot

police officer

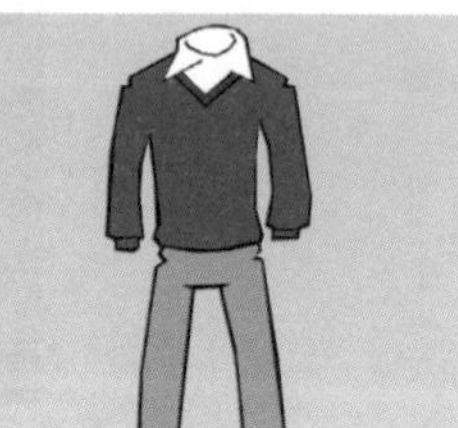
uniform

Can you think of five more jobs?

World of work

factory

fire engine

fire station

meeting

news

newspaper

office

police station

Which work places are in your town?

Things in the home

brush

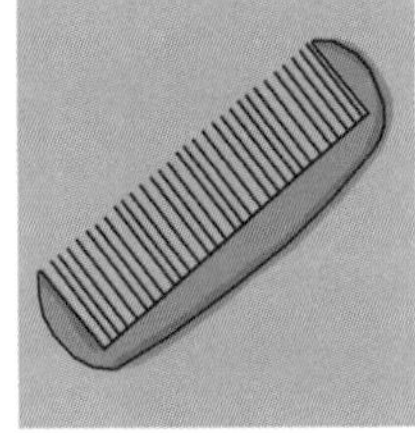
comb

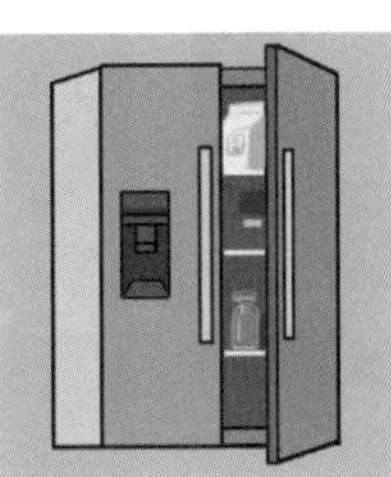
fridge

gate

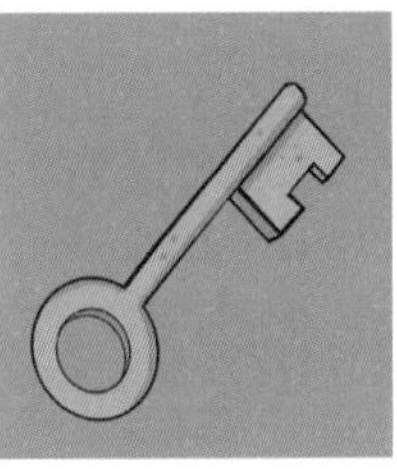
key

oven

shampoo

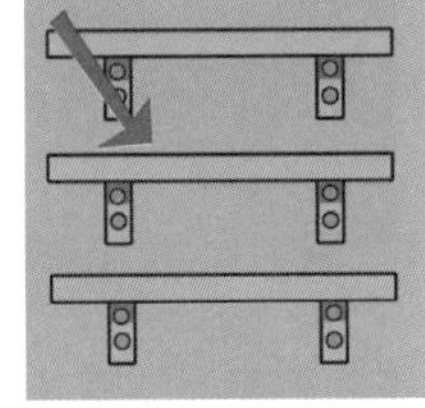
shelf

soap

telephone

toilet

Where can you find these things at home?

Adjectives to describe objects

broken

cheap

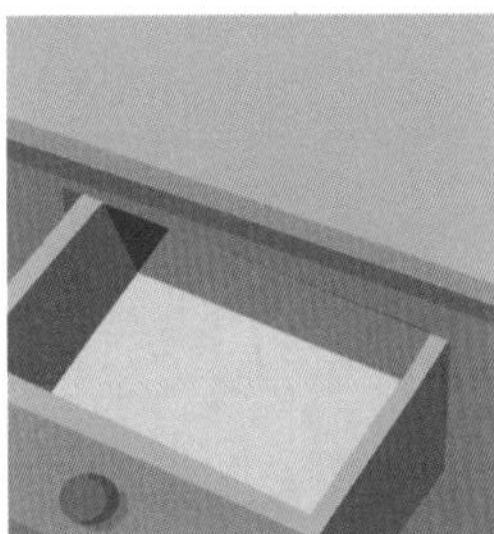
empty

expensive

full

heavy

light

tidy

untidy

unusual

Think of an object, place or animal for each adjective.

In space

astronaut

deep

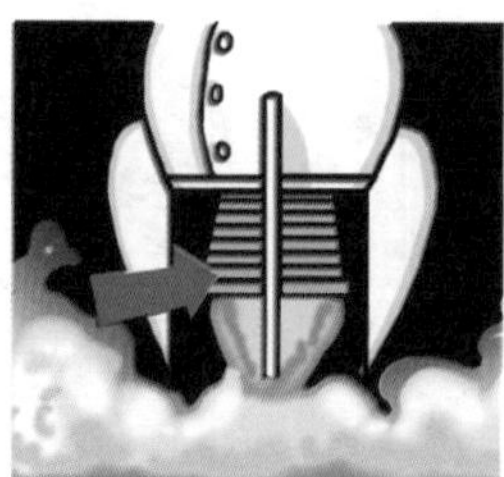
engine

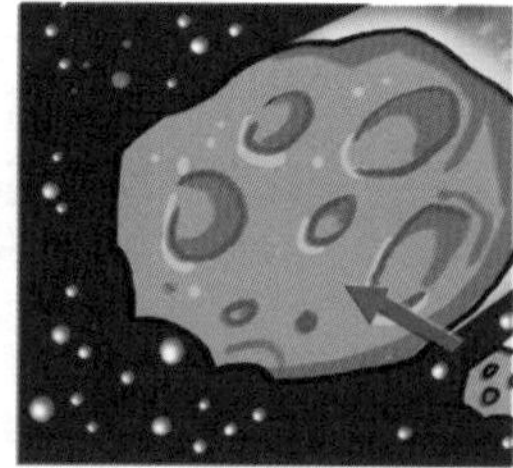
enormous

frightening

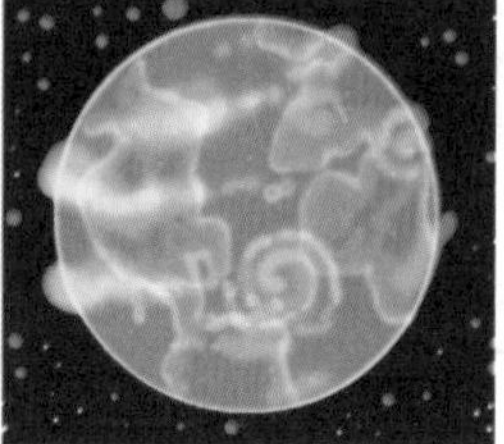
planet

rocket

space

spaceship

telescope

Which space word is also a job?

Adventure verbs

enter

entrance

exit

follow

land

save

stay

touch

turn off

turn on

Choose five verbs. How do you do them?

Mealtimes and snacks

delicious

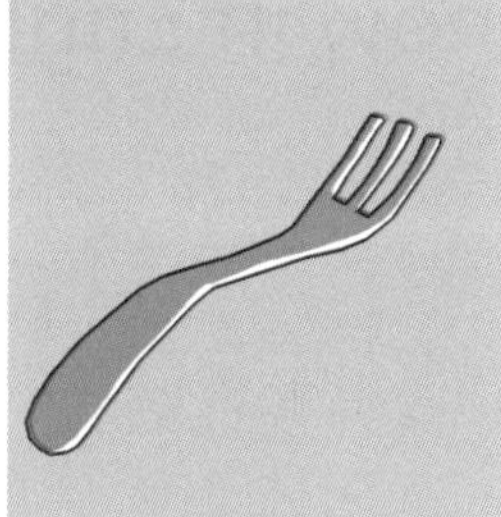

fork

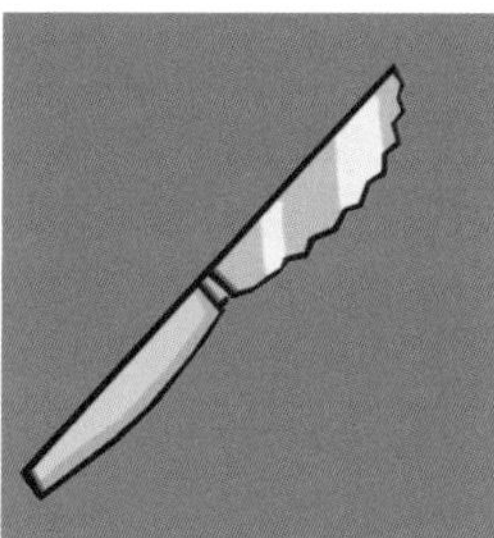

knife

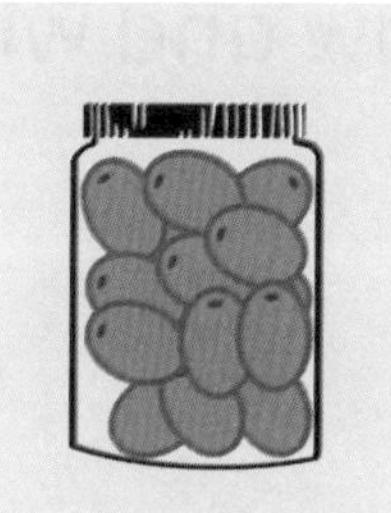

olives

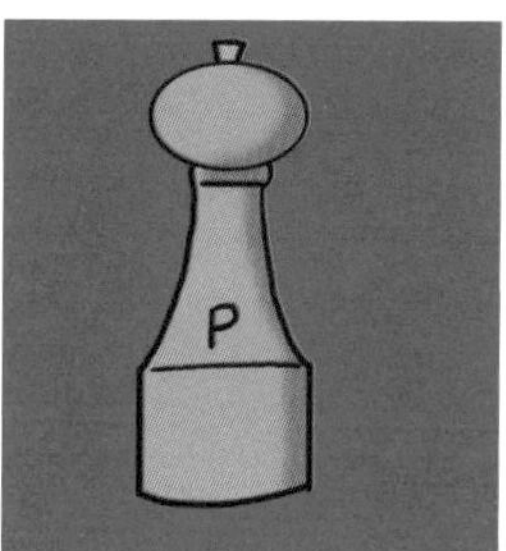

pepper

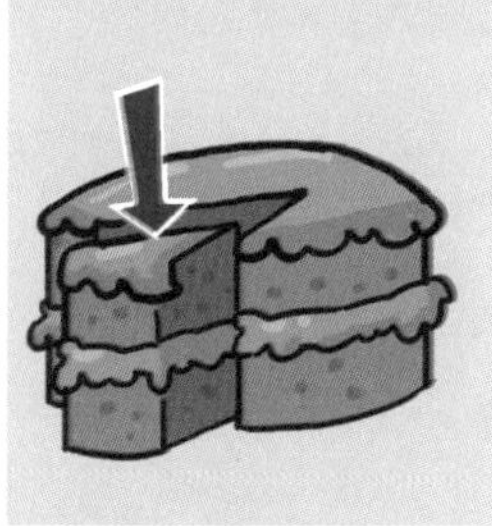

piece

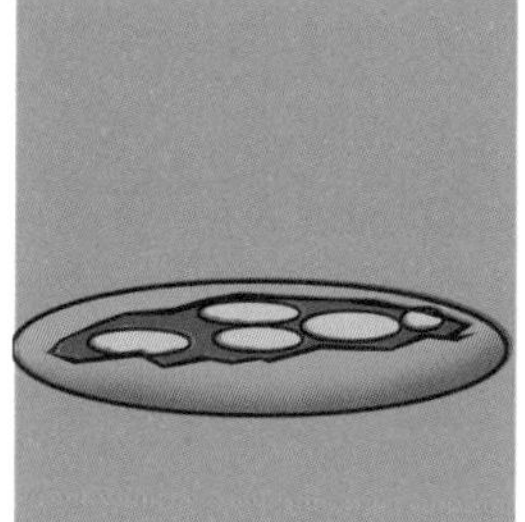

pizza

salt

snacks

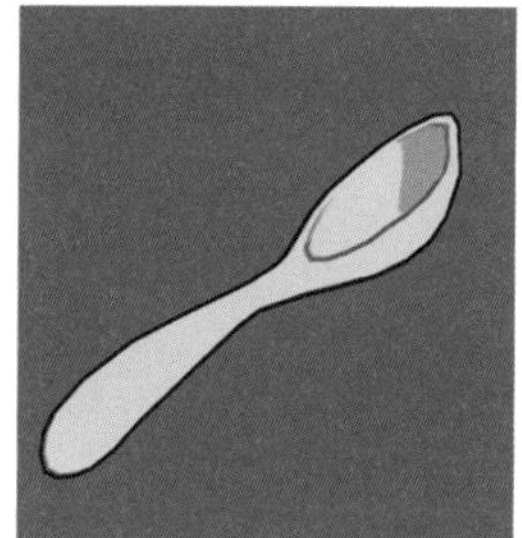

spoon

What are your favourite snacks?

Cooking

bake

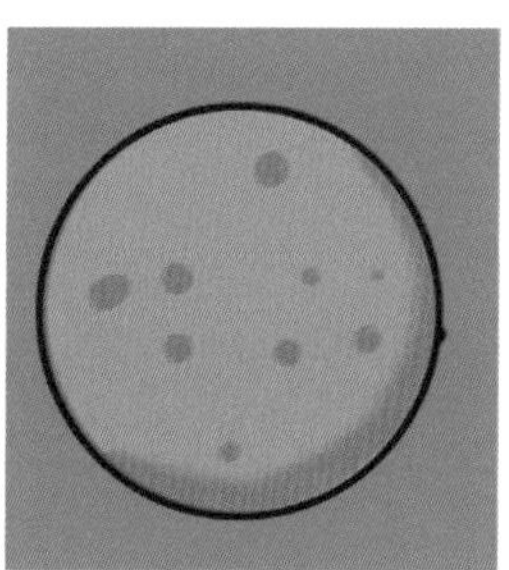

biscuit

butter

cooker

egg

flour

honey

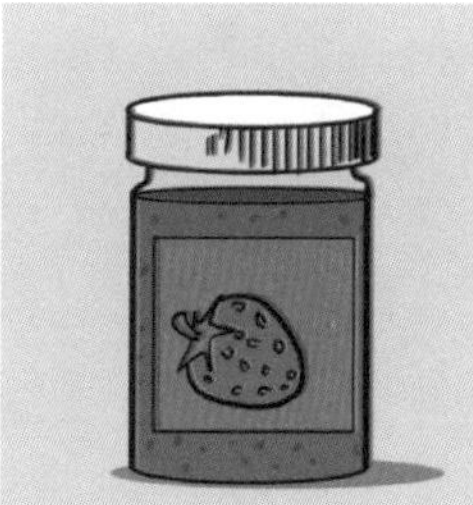

jam

sugar

wash up

What do you need to make biscuits? Say five things.

Draw and write words you know in English.

My picture dictionary

Draw and write words you know in English.